CONFLICTS

A BETTER WAY TO RESOLVE THEM

CONFLICTS

A BETTER WAY TO RESOLVE THEM

Edward de Bono

HARRAP   LONDON

First published in Great Britain 1985
by HARRAP LIMITED
19–23 Ludgate Hill, London EC4M 7PD

© *European Music Ltd* 1985

ISBN 0 245-54322-8

Design by Tina Dutton; design and production in association with Book Production Consultants, Cambridge

Typesetting by Witwell Ltd., Liverpool

Printed and bound by Butler and Tanner, Frome, Somerset

CONTENTS

PROLOGUE

We do have to accept that our methods of solving major disputes and conflicts have been crude and primitive, inadequate and expensive, dangerous and destructive. The increasing complexity of the world and the increasing power of our weaponry force us to rethink our conflict-solving methods.

Even if we were to operate our traditional methods with the best will in the world and with the highest available intelligence, these methods would not suffice. There is a need for a fundamental shift in our thinking approach to the resolution of conflicts.

In this book I do not presume to set down an instant answer but I intend to indicate a road along which, I believe, we must travel. I shall go further and indicate some of the first steps that can be taken.

Amongst these first steps is a reappraisal of our esteemed argument/clash type of thinking. I shall attempt to point out the attractions, dangers and limitations of this traditional method. I shall suggest that conflict thinking about conflict is inadequate and that we must shift to the 'design' type of thinking with its creative input.

I find no villains but intelligent people locked by the logic and continuity of their positions into the argument/clash mode. It is unfortunate that the parties most directly involved in a dispute may be in the worst position to settle the dispute — this is as if the Bondi Beach lifeguards were all unable to swim.

There are three roads to conflict resolution: fight/litigate; negotiate/bargain; design a way out. Only the first two are available to the disputants. The design road demands a third party that can look at the situation from the third party angle. For this reason I introduce the concept of 'triangular thinking'. This third party is neither judge nor negotiator but a creative designer.

You can propel a heavy ball across a sponge surface by pushing the ball —or by depressing the surface just ahead of the ball, thus leading it forward.

That has always been the power of ideas.

We do have to accept that our methods of solving disputes and conflicts are crude and primitive, inadequate and costly, dangerous and destructive.

Even if we operate these methods with the best will in the world and with the highest intelligence, they will not suffice. There is a need for a fundamental shift in our approach to the resolution of conflicts.

INTRODUCTION

An Aztec priest slices open the chest of the living victim with a knife made of lava glass. The victim is held arched backwards over a stone altar in order to separate the ribs. The priest plunges in his hand, tears out the victim's heart and holds it aloft. The heart continues to pulsate and squirm in the priest's hands. The discarded victim's body is tossed down the steps of the pyramid.

From our standpoint today that behavior may seem cruel and primitive. From the standpoint of that time, the behavior was glorious and noble and most enthusiastic (in the true sense of that word: 'with God').

Can we conceive a time when our descendants will look back in just such a manner, to regard as cruel and primitive the way in which we now seek to solve disputes and conflicts by killing people on rather a large scale? The technological sophistication with which that is carried out will not disguise the primitiveness of the underlying principle.

The next and last war is logically inevitable. I use the word 'last' both in the horrific sense of considerable destruction and also in the logical sense of the 'last' of a series.

There was a time when family fought family. Then tribe fought tribe. City fought city in Greece and later in Italy. Then nations became the fighting units. As weapons increased in power so the units became bigger. As the expense of war increased only bigger units could afford it. As communication technology improved, cultures and values became more uniform. In Europe today it would be unthinkable for England to declare war on France or for Germany to attack Austria. Yet, less than a lifetime ago, wars on this scale were very thinkable. The superpower bloc is the next logical progression. After that the technology of communication, the interlocking of economies and the cost of war should make the idiom obsolete on any major scale.

Do we have to proceed through this logical inevitability or can we bypass it?

Consider a heavy S.K.F. ball-bearing suspended by a cord directly above a delicate Baccarat crystal goblet. The cord is on fire. There is a certain logical inevitability that the glass is due to be shattered. The components are in place and if they work out their destiny according to present behavior the ball will fall on the glass and shatter it. Something untoward might happen: a breeze may extinguish the fire. If you owned that glass would you wait for something unexpected to rescue the glass or would you want to be rather more constructive?

In a similar way all the pieces are in place for disastrous conflicts up to and including nuclear war. There is the logic of weapon technology and the logic of armament competition. There is the logic of deterrence. There is tension and hostility and lack of communication. There are crude and primitive ways of handling this through institutions like the United Nations, which is structurally inadequate for the role. There are very old-fashioned concepts and idioms of thinking which work to inflame conflict rather than design a way out of it.

We cannot conceive of new concepts until after we have conceived of them.

For thousands of years the great civilizations of Egypt, Carthage, Greece and Rome were unable to measure time. They had adequate technology in the water clock — but they lacked a very simple concept. These civilizations tried to divide daytime into equal hours and night-time, separately, into equal hours. Since a Mediterranean latitude meant that day and night were always varying in length, the task was very difficult. It was only when man hit on the simple concept of dividing up the whole twenty-four hours that timekeeping became simple: an obvious concept that took a long time to come through. Could there be concepts just as basic to which we are complacently blind?

I have written before that the most hopeful thing about the human race is its relative stupidity.

If I had to believe that humanity was operating at the full throttle of its intellectual potential and still producing the crises, mess and dangers of today's world, then there could be little hope. In this book I aim to be more hopeful by considering precisely this fortunate stupidity of the human race.

Why is it that our intelligence has locked us into habits, idioms and institutions that prevent a better use of our intelligence?

The reason is that we have developed a thinking system that was appropriate when developed but is now dangerously inadequate. That thinking system has served us well in most areas — except the area of conflict resolution, where it is totally useless. This is because the thinking system (based on language logic and the principle of contradiction) is itself a conflict method. So we apply conflict to the solution of conflict.

We now know enough about how the brain works to be able to design more suitable thinking systems. In particular we know that perception is a self-organizing information system that is quite different from our usual 'passive' information systems. For lack of such understanding we have never been able to work in the important perceptual area but have had to work in the downstream area of a logic (or mathematics) which can only work on perceptions that have already been formed.

It is in this perceptual area that creativity and design get to work.

In this book I am going to show that our much revered thinking systems are old-fashioned, inadequate and dangerous when it comes to conflict resolution. We need to substitute the constructive 'design idiom' rather than the dialectic argument system that is so much the basis of our civilization. We need to jettison the principle of contradiction in order to use new logics.

In any dispute the two opposing parties are logically incapable of designing a way out. There is a fundamental need for a third party role. That leads to the concept of 'triangular thinking' which I shall be introducing.

Our present structures of governments and the United Nations are structurally inadequate to take on the design role. With the best will in the world they will remain representative and argumentative. There is a clearly defined need for a new organization which will have a supranational independent thinking role. This is S.I.T.O. and I shall explain how it will work.

I want to make it clear that I am not going to adopt the traditional complainer's role of attacking a system and pointing out its faults, in the hope that correction of such faults will put things right. There cannot be any hope of that. Changes within the same idiom cannot work. There has to be a change of idiom. So I shall be pointing out the inadequacies of our present thinking and structures for conflict resolution and then offering practical alternatives.

The needed shift is much more fundamental than most people realize. Our thinking systems are desperately old-fashioned no matter with what complacency and pride we hold them. They are totally inadequate for conflict resolution. You will never get to talk Spanish through improving the way you speak French. There needs to be a language shift.

But this is not a book of exhortation or complaint. The book puts forward a practical idiom for conflict thinking: the design idiom. The book also puts forward a practical supranational structure for conflict thinking: S.I.T.O.

Edward de Bono   Palazzo Marnisi
                                                 Marsaxlokk, Malta

CONFLICT

A clash of interests, values, actions or directions. Conflict refers to the existence of that clash. The word conflict is applicable from the instant that the clash occurs. Even when we say that there is a potential conflict we are implying that there is already a conflict of direction even though a clash may not yet have occurred.

CONFLICTION

This is a new word. Its meaning is fairly obvious. Confliction is the process of setting up, promoting, encouraging or designing conflict. Note that confliction refers to the actual effort put into creating a conflict. It covers all those deliberate things which happen before the conflict is established. Confliction is meant to refer to a deliberate process. It is the effort to establish a conflict. We do not have to be concerned here with why anyone would want to establish a conflict.

DE-CONFLICTION

This is also a new word I am inventing. De-confliction is even more important than confliction. In order for de-confliction to make sense we need to have the word 'confliction'. De-confliction is the opposite of confliction. It refers to the designing away or dissipation of the basis for the conflict. De-confliction does not refer to negotiation or bargaining or even to the resolution of conflicts. De-confliction is the effort required to evaporate a conflict. Just as confliction is the setting up of a conflict so de-confliction is the opposite process: the demolition of the conflict.

This book is about de-confliction.

PART I THE WAY THE MIND WORKS AND MODES OF THINKING

CHAPTER 1

WHY WE NEED TO KNOW HOW THE MIND WORKS

There is a horrific story about the lady who put her wet and shivering poodle into the microwave oven to dry out. I doubt if the story is true but the point it makes is important: you need to know how a system works.

Let me say at this point that I believe that it can never be enough ever again to consider the outcome of human thinking without considering the nature of human thinking.

Human thinking is information activity in that special environment that we call the brain. We do not yet know the detailed workings of the brain but we do have a broad view of the type of information system that it is. From this broad view we can take practical and definite types of information behavior and we can apply these principles directly to human thinking.

You may protest that millions of people drive motor cars very well indeed without having the faintest idea of how an internal combustion engine works. So why do we need to understand the brain in order to use it effectively? The answer is that someone who understands internal combustion engines very well indeed has designed the engine, its reliability and the simplified controls. Furthermore, if anything goes wrong you just hand the problem over to the mechanic. The point is that someone understands the system and that is why it is designed to be efficient and practical. With regards to our minds we are just about reaching that stage.

It is quite true that we have excellent systems of mathematics and logic. We are rapidly building up great expertise in computer hardware and software. These are all second-stage thinking processes.

The first stage of thinking is perception. It is in perception that the chaos of the external world is translated into symbols or words which can then be manipulated in the excellent second-stage systems we have invented. Such systems can be highly artificial and bear no resemblance whatever to the way the brain actually works. But *perception itself* depends directly on the way the brain works. That is why we have been so very poor at dealing with perception: because we have not understood the system involved. As I shall explain shortly we are now beginning to understand perception as a 'self-organizing information system'. This is quite different from the information systems that we have been used to.

Most of our thinking is language based. Such language-based thinking systems are also second-stage systems. We inherit words and over time our experience may allow new words to form. The rules for handling the words are laid down by grammar and usage. We are very proud of our language-based thinking system and we believe it to be rather wonderful — which it is. It is the only game in town and our culture is so dependent on language-based thinking that we cannot really conceive of anything else.

Yet language-based thinking has some very serious deficiencies and dangers. This is especially so when it comes to conflict thinking, which is what this book is about. By its nature, language-based thinking tends to give distinctions, separations and categories. This is hardly surprising since this is the very purpose of language. Language-based thinking tends to give identity and permanent labels. From such things comes the logic associated with language-based thinking. This is a logic based on identity, equivalence, enclosure and — above all — the principle of contradiction. As I shall explain in the course of this book, all these aspects have had a profoundly negative effect on conflict thinking.

How else could we think? Imagine a planet going about its proper business. It is constantly passing through different relationships, transition phases and temporary states. There is constant flow and change in contrast with the categorization and permanence of language-based thinking. In part mathematics approaches this other sort of thinking. So does cybernetics. But both are somewhat primitive and limited for general use.

For the time being we shall have to go on using language-based thinking, as I shall do myself in the course of this book. We can, however, take three steps to mitigate the dangerous limitations of language-based thinking (as a matter of interest these limitations apply more to prose than to poetry). The three steps are as follows.

1. Understand the nature of perception.
2. Be aware of the dangers of language.
3. Introduce some new devices into language (for example the new word 'po' which I invented some years ago, and will discuss later).

THE NATURE OF PERCEPTION

Take three men, each of whom is holding in his hand a small piece of wood. Each man lets go of this piece of wood.

In the case of the first man the wood falls downwards.

In the case of the second man the wood goes upwards.

In the case of the third man the wood remains just where it is.

The behavior of the wood in the first case is perfectly normal, logical and expected. The behavior of the wood in the other two cases is bizarre, extraordinary and completely unbelievable. But this is only because we expect the second and third man to be in the same *universe of action* as the first man.

The universe of action is the system or set of circumstances in which something is taking place. For example, all of Euclid's geometry took place in the universe of a plane two-dimensional surface. In such a universe the angles of a triangle do always add up to 180 degrees. As soon as we change the universe from a plane surface to a spherical one then Euclid's theorems may not hold: for example the angles of a triangle now add up to more than 180 degrees.

We expect all three men to be standing on the surface of the earth in a normal way. Try as we might we cannot explain the strange behavior of the second and third pieces of wood in this 'normal' universe. The mystery is instantly solved when I explain that the three universes are different. In the first case the man is standing on the surface of the earth so the wood falls downwards in the expected manner. In the second case he is standing under water and in this different universe the wood naturally floats upwards. In the third case the man is in an orbiting space-craft so the weightless wood remains just where it is.

In this simple example we can see how strange and unexplainable behavior suddenly becomes obvious and logical — once we have understood that it is taking place in a *different universe*.

This point is an extremely important one. The reason we have not understood perception is that we have always assumed that perception takes place in the same sort of information universe as writing or drawing. We are used to 'passive' information universes in which you make marks on a piece of paper or a magnetic disk and those marks remain where they are placed. The information universe of perception is quite different: it is an 'active' information universe.

CROSSING THE ROAD

If you take a simple three-by-three grid and place the number one in any box and then the number two in any box, and so on until all nine numbers have been placed, you will find that there are rather a large number of ways in which the numbers can be distributed. In fact the number is 362,880 different ways. This is just a simple way of illustrating that the mathematics of combination give huge figures.

If, as you stood waiting to cross the road, your brain had to try out all incoming information in different combinations in order to recognize the traffic conditions, it would take you at least a month to cross the road. In fact the changing conditions would make it impossible for you ever to cross.

It is quite obvious that in perception the brain has to make very rapid sense of the world around. That is where 'active information systems' come in. Such systems allow incoming information to organize itself into *patterns*.

Once such a pattern is formed then all that is required is a single input that triggers that pattern. In this way we 'recognize' the scene and cross the road in normal human time. Life would be utterly impossible without this pattern-making and pattern-using nature of perception. That is the very purpose of perception. It is an immensely *useful* fundamental aspect of mind and computer scientists would dearly love to get their machines to do it as well. Nevertheless this pattern making inevitably gives rise to rigidity and stereotypes. That is why there is such a great need for the creativity and lateral thinking that I shall be describing later in this book.

ACTIVE INFORMATION SYSTEMS

Imagine a towel laid on a table. From a nearby bowl a spoonful of ink is taken and poured on to the towel. An ink stain results. At the end the towel carries an accurate record of the placings of the spoonfuls of ink. This is a typical 'passive' information surface: like making marks on paper or magnetic tape.

Let us now contrast an 'active' surface. Instead of the towel there is a shallow dish of gelatin (Jell-O). This time the bowl of ink is heated on a small fire. When the spoonful of hot ink is poured on to the surface the hot ink melts the gelatin. When the cooled ink and melted gelatin is poured off, a small depression is left in the surface. This corresponds to the ink stain on the towel.

The same placement and sequence of spoonfuls is now put on to the gelatin surface (with a pouring off of fluid between each). At the end there would be a channel eroded in the gelatin surface. This is because the ink in the second spoonful would spread on the surface and if this spread overlapped the first depression the ink would flow into this. At the end a channel would be formed.

The gelatin model is a very simple example of an environment which allows incoming information to organize itself into a 'pattern'. In short, it is a 'self-organizing information system'.

By a pattern we mean a channel so that once we enter at one end of the channel then we flow along to the other end. By that we mean a sequence in time so that a succession of states follow one after the other — just as if they were strung out along a channel.

There is, of course, a very much simpler example of a self-organizing information system in the ordinary landscape. The early arriving rain forms little streams which then join to form rivulets and finally rivers. Once these 'patterns' have formed then all future rainfall has to follow these paths.

From the point of view of the mind this is a fantastic system. It is a system that makes sense out of chaos. It is a system that allows very rapid recognition and reaction.

THE MECHANISM OF MIND

It is possible to show how nerve networks in the brain can behave as self-organizing information systems. I wrote all this up in 1969 in a book called 'The Mechanism of Mind' (still published by Penguin Books Ltd., London). That book was instrumental in changing the education system of Venezuela in a significant way (through Dr Luis Alberto Machado). The model put forward in the book has been simulated on computer and does behave largely as predicted.

The book was largely ignored at the time and yet today the behavior of 'self-organizing information systems' is the growing wave at the front edge of information technology. There is no doubt at all in my mind that very big advances will be made in this direction. My own ideas have gone much further than those expressed in 'The Mechanism of Mind' and I should write a new version one day.

What is important si that we do not need to wait to know all the details of the working of the brain in order to make useful deductions from the likely type of system.

The behavior of self-organizing patterning systems seems simple and obvious but the implications are profound and very far reaching. For instance, it becomes obvious that humor is the most significant characteristic of the human mind. Humor tells us more about the information behavior of mind than does anything else.

We can prove how traditional philosophers were not concerned with the perceptual aspect of thinking by their neglect of the importance of humor. Philosophers have traditionally been playing word games. The time has come to look at the system basis of thinking.

I am well aware that much of what I have written so far in this section may be repetitive to someone who knows my work well. I am caught in a dilemma. I cannot omit what is so crucial a part of my mission without leaving it suspended without a base. I cannot assume that any reader of this book will have read a previous book such as 'The Mechanism of Mind'. So I have no choice other than to ask the forgiveness of those who know my work — and to ask them to pay special attention to new aspects that I may not have mentioned before.

THE IMPLICATIONS

As I have said, the implications of an understanding of the self-organizing nature of perception are considerable.

Once we can understand patterns and particularly the asymmetric nature of patterns (which I shall come to in a later section) then we can understand both humor and creativity. We can go further and design deliberate creative tools that can be used in a practical manner.

We can also understand a most extraordinary cultural dilemma to do with creativity. I shall discuss it in detail later in the section on creativity, but I shall mention it briefly here. The dilemma is this. Any valuable creative idea must always be logical in hindsight. Therefore we have always felt that what is needed is better logic rather than creativity. This is a complete and very tragic misunderstanding of the system. It is an almost perfect example of the dangers that arise when a system is not understood. As we shall see later there are very good reasons why something may *only* be obvious logically in hindsight.

An understanding of the nature of perception also has profound implications for our operation of the 'scientific method'. Traditionally we form the most reasonable hypothesis and then (if we follow Karl Popper) set about refuting that hypothesis in order to change it for a better one. There is a very serious fault in this. Whilst we hold an hypothesis, however reasonable, we can only see the evidence as structured — perceptually by that hypothesis. In other words, much of the evidence in front of us is invisible to us. That is why it often happens in science that the evidence for a new theory is eventually found to have been available a long time before. But it could never be seen because vision was structured by the 'reasonable hypothesis'. As a simple start we could suggest that there should never be just one hypothesis — no matter how dominant or reasonable. There must always be at least one other — no matter how unlikely — to provide an alternative structuring. There are other implications which affect how strongly a subject should be researched before it is thought about. Too much research makes innovation more difficult. There are huge areas that need re-thinking and where the answer may be very different from the traditional one.

Later on in the book I shall be dealing with perception and the belief system. The reality of beliefs is quite different from experience reality or scientific reality, and yet it is every bit as real. Clearly the nature of belief reality has a highly significant impact on conflict thinking since so many conflicts arise from just such clashes of belief.

MOOD

We come now to an area which is rather more speculative than the preceding areas. But it is an area of rather great importance and with rather upsetting implications. There is beginning to be a hint of research evidence for it. On a theoretical base (information systems) there is a very strong case for it and I would predict that scientific findings will eventually prove it to be so.

The ancient Greeks had a quaint and naive belief that moods were controlled by bodily fluids. If you were in a bad mood then it was because your body was suffused with 'black bile' — hence the word melancholy.

Well, they may have been right. We are beginning to know a lot more about the complex and subtle part that chemicals play in the brain. This is in addition to their role as transmitters that allow a nerve impulse to cross from one nerve to another. It seems that there are various neuro-peptide messengers which can then split into further messengers and so on. Such messengers might inhibit or make easier nerve activity at specific places. So we get a complex and altering chemical background against which the neural behavior takes place.

On a theoretical basis, any self-organizing system suffers from rigidity because that is the purpose for which it was designed. A particular neural state will follow along the pattern sequence into a predetermined state without fail. Let us now suppose that the bathing chemical background alters. The same initial neural state might now find itself followed by quite a different state. Under those chemical circumstances that would always be the case. It is as if there was a different brain present with the different chemical background. At once the flexibility and richness of the system is greatly improved. Behavior may also be more appropriate.

In everyday terms these chemical settings are what we may call emotions (there are probably others as well which we do not yet recognize as emotions). It is an interesting thought that when we really start designing intelligent computers we may well have to give them 'emotions'.

Of course, we all know that emotions affect people's thinking. But it is much more fundamental than that. It is not a matter of a person choosing the thoughts that fit his or her emotion of the moment. It may be that in that emotional state a thinker is simply *incapable* of having certain types of thought. It is not a matter of choice. That thinker would be just as incapable of having those thoughts as a person who had never been to New York would be incapable of recollecting his New York experiences. The chemically different brain may temporarily be a *different* brain. The implications of this for ethics are enormous. So are the implications for conflict thinking.

I remember a depressed person writing to me to tell me his observation that he found that when he was depressed he was incapable of having the same thoughts that he had when he was elated. It was not just that he chose not to have them or did not find such thoughts turning up.

BACK-UP

For the moment let us put aside the step-by-step logic that works through a mathematical problem to an answer. In such cases, once the world has been translated into symbols then the rules of symbol behavior take over. Let us look at all those situations which we cannot yet adequately translate into symbols and delegate to symbol-manipulating computers (it hardly needs me to remind the reader of the great danger of a spurious translation of the world into symbols and then a totally false confidence in the result because the maths were right).

We know a lot more about what is called 'right-brain' thinking. This is contrasted with 'left-brain' thinking which is essentially language and symbolic thinking. In left-brain thinking attention can focus in on a detail and isolate it. In right-brain thinking there is a whole pattern or general impression that cannot be broken down into parts. For that reason it can be reacted to but not described or communicated — except perhaps by art. It may simply be that right-brain experience is just more primitive and has not had a chance to connect up and differentiate. It does not matter.

Suppose that our emotions and our general right brain 'impression' always set the end-point of our thinking and that when we believe ourselves to be thinking something through it *can only be* a process of 'back-up' or rationalization.

On theoretical grounds it is extremely likely that in a system like the brain thinking always starts backwards. It is possible to predict and show that learning occurs much more easily backwards.

Supposing I were to put forward the notion — only as a provocation at this stage — that it was physiologically impossible for someone to think something through logically? When we think we are doing so we are only fooling ourselves with the tidiness and coherence of our output.

SUMMARY

This is, of course, the most important section of the book. Nevertheless the rest of the book will make sense in its own right if a reader does not understand, does not accept or does not believe what I have put forward. At the other extreme will be the reader who will read between the lines and who will understand important implications that I have only hinted at.

This is the summary. We have developed excellent second-stage thinking systems which can handle symbols once perception has translated the world into such symbols. Much of the important part of thinking (especially in conflicts) takes place in the perception area. We need to understand perception as a self-organizing pattern-making system. This is an 'active system' quite different from the 'passive' information systems to which we are used. Very many implications arise from the behavior of patterning systems.

Our word-based thinking system has many serious limitations — especially categorization and permanence. Indeed our whole confidence in our thinking system may well be misplaced.

Why then has the system served us reasonably well? The answer is that it has not. It has served us very badly indeed. To be sure it has served us well when we are dealing with second-stage thinking and with finite objects. It has also served us well when we are dealing with perception in an 'open situation' because it does not matter too much how we structure things. It has served us very badly when dealing with perception in closed situations where there can be clashes of perceptions and beliefs. Our record in such areas is appalling. This is what we would expect.

CHAPTER 2

WHAT IS WRONG WITH ARGUMENT

A rgument is the most venerated of Western thinking traditions. Much of civilization is based upon it: for example government and the courts. Whether we call it argument, debate, dialectic or clash it comes to the same thing.

I am going to use this section to attack the very essence of 'argument'. I shall do so vehemently and the paradox is that I shall probably be using the argument mode to attack argument itself.

Let me say that I do see quite a lot of merit in the argument method. I am forced, however, by the normal polarization of dialectic to attack it as if it was worthless and dangerous. As a matter of fact I believe that it is dangerous but not worthless.

An inadequately trained doctor — innocent of his ignorance — delivers the wrong medication and kills the patient. He is not a murderer. He is not evil. He is not a monster. But his innocent inadequacy can have the same effects. That is very much what I feel about the argument mode. I feel it is overvenerated and overused. I believe it is used with innocence because it feels good and useful and because there is no obvious alternative. Nevertheless the method is dangerous by reason of its inadequacy, and because the false feeling of adequacy can prevent the development of much better methods.

I do not want to get into the historic development of the argument method. It goes back to the Socratic dialogue which seems to have been more tetchy challenge than gentle exploration. The method was adopted and refined by the Church thinkers of the Middle Ages because it suited their purposes exactly. They needed a powerful method to repel the numerous heretics. To some extent the system was a closed one inasmuch as the basic concepts of God, eternity, justice and perfection (amongst others) were commonly held. This is an ideal — and legitimate — setting for semantic type argument. A good job was done even though St Augustine occasionally needed to rescue himself by inventing matters like 'divine grace' when he was losing an argument. The Church set the tone for Western thinking, culture and education and so the argument tradition was solidly bedded. There were many other reasons including the employment the mode gave to philosophers.

It hardly needs saying that the argument idiom has always been the mainstay of conflict thinking and is itself a model of conflict thinking.

HOW ARGUMENT IS SUPPOSED TO WORK

There is an idea which needs changing. There is an idea you believe to be wrong. There is a case, a claim, a point of view or an activity which you wish to oppose. So you set up to attack what is being presented. There is the thesis and you bring forth the antithesis.

From the ferment and clash of battle there is supposed to emerge the 'synthesis' which combines the best of both. It would be absurd for me to say this never happens, but it very rarely happens. It is not hard to see why it rarely happens. There is very little action or motivation on the part of either thinker to pick out the best in the opposite view. At best the synthesis is a grudging compromise or a retreat from a position.

In theory thesis and antithesis have always had an attractiveness based on neatness and activity. In practice this usually does not work. It may sometimes work in science, although the history of science is full of useless battles that were fought in defense of old-fashioned ideas.

What usually happens is that one or other side triumphs and the other is defeated — in a simple trial-of-strength idiom. The end result is the strength of a point of view, not the excellence of that view.

Before we get to this point of triumph and defeat we must watch what is happening to the combatants.

The defender gets very much more rigid and more definite about what is being defended. All exploratory tentacles are withdrawn. The rigidity gets worse.

The attacker gets more strident and more fierce. He also has to become more focused and cannot afford explorations.

We might summarize the points as follows.

1. Each side gets more rigid.
2. Neither side makes an attempt to develop an idea different from the two that are clashing.
3. An indefinite amount of time, energy and cost are locked up in a stand-off which may continue for a long time.

4. The creativity and ingenuity of each side is not directed at improving their idea but in securing the defeat of the opposing idea.
5. At the end the idea which triumphs is the stronger but not necessarily the better idea.

The main objection is that all the creative energy is not being used to develop better ideas.

AN EXPLORATION IDIOM

The idiom that I shall describe here has something in common with the Japanese idiom but is rather idealized. It should not derive any virtue because of an alleged Japanese flavor: it should make sense in its own right.

The Japanese simply did not develop the Western dialectic habit. For a long time Japan was a feudal society full of protocol, respect and manners. It would be extremely bad manners to tell a person that he was wrong or his idea incorrect. It might even have been criminal to suggest that something ought to be changed. So the verbal attack idiom never seemed to have emerged.

'That is wonderful and perfect and cannot be improved — now let's explore.'

To the Western mind that seems a contradiction, because if something is wonderful and perfect, then what is the point in exploring?

In a later section I shall come to the difficulties created by the Western concept of contradiction which is so much at the basis of our language logic. For the moment let us pursue the Japanese idiom unperturbed by the apparent contradiction.

So *both parties* now undertake the exploration. Both parties are looking for better ideas. Both parties are interested in seeing the good points in the ideas of the other. In short there is an exploration instead of an argument.

It is worth noting that in an argument stand-off the amount of time taken up in the stand-off is almost totally unproductive. In the exploration idiom the amount of time taken for exploration is totally productive.

Should the joint exploration result in an idea which both parties like then there can be a sudden switch to that idea. The old idea is left unchallenged and undemolished — but no longer used. As a matter of interest, our understanding of perception suggests that the best way to get rid of an idea is to ignore it — attacking it only makes it more real.

We come now to a most interesting phenomenon which has great relevance for Western society. If the Japanese explorers *do not* find a better idea then they simply return to the old idea which has been quite unmolested and has been grazing quietly in the meadow. Contrast this with the dialectic idiom in which the full force of thinking is turned to destroying and discrediting the old idea. If this is achieved and there is no alternative idea available then society is suspended in chaos, having thoroughly destroyed the old base and yet not turned its thinking to devise a new one. It is a totally absurd Western thinking idiom that attack is a sufficient generative and design system.

There is yet a further advantage to the Japanese system. In the Western system you cannot really ask for a change until you have in some way shown the inadequacy of what exists. There are many things which are worthwhile and cannot be shown to be wrong: for example this applies to many school subjects which are valuable in their own right but do take up time which could be more usefully employed. It is obvious that in the Japanese system you can look at something which is really good and still try to improve it. It is precisely that idiom that gave rise to Japanese quality and Quality Circles.

I want to make it clear that I am not singing the praises of the Japanese culture as such. In order to show that our 'clash' system is only one particular way of proceeding, I need to show a system which did not have the dialectic tradition. The Japanese did have wars, conflicts and clashes based on the same power, greed and selfishness as everyone else. But because they did not have the dialectic thinking tradition they are further along the 'design road' that I put forward in this book.

At this point I am usually challenged in the following way: if the Japanese are so good at change why do they seem so poor at invention and scientific breakthroughs? The Japanese are good at the small concept jump and what they call 'combination invention', but not so good at the major concept leap. This is because the major concept leap requires a 'bloody-minded' individual who pursues his own local logic oblivious to the condemnation of those around him. When Frank Whittle set out to design the jet engine his colleagues scoffed at the idea — but he persisted and succeeded. Marconi was born in Italy but lived in England long enough to become bloody-minded. As a physicist he knew that radio waves would follow a straight line and would not follow the curve of the earth. Nevertheless he set out to transmit wireless signals from Newfoundland to Cornwall. His friends called him mad. He was merely bloody-minded. He succeeded because the ionosphere reflected the wireless waves back to earth. Bloody-mindedness is a form of local logic which makes sense only to the person or persons holding that logic — but not to those around. In England it is equally responsible for a high rate of inventiveness and a high rate of industrial unrest. In a group culture like Japan such individual bloody-mindedness could not occur because if your colleagues believed you to be mad you shut up.

Surely the Western dialectic system is responsible for our technical progress. Surely the clash of theory and counter-theory is the very essence of our technical progress. I believe this has played only a small part. The key to Western technology development is the concept of the 'hypothesis' — the speculation about what might be that leads thinking forward into exploration. Chinese technology was very far advanced many centuries ago. This was when the technicians were experimenting and trying things out. Then it got into the hands of the scholars and academics who explained everything and removed any need for experimentation. Chinese technology never developed the concept of the hypothesis so it came to an abrupt stop. It has been said that the West developed the hypothesis because of a belief in God. This leads to the notion that God has a hidden design for the world. An hypothesis is a guess at this design. Chinese culture was never theistic and so with no God there was no hidden design to be guessed at — so no hypothesis.

We shall see later how both the individual bloody-mindedness and the general concept of the hypothesis can be captured in a deliberate and formal manner in the provocative aspects of lateral thinking. Indeed the 'po' concept allows a temporary and controllable form of insanity which allows the thinker to transcend the logical relationships of any idea in order to find a new idea.

Let us now list the main points about the 'exploration idiom'.

1. The existing idea is not attacked and may be returned to later without having suffered any discredit or damage.
2. From the beginning both parties are involved in creative exploration and design.
3. The whole time is taken up in a positive and creative manner.
4. Since there is no need to show fault it is possible to set out to change an idea which is already good.
5. The idea is jointly designed and then jointly evaluated.
6. There is not the problem of 'ownership': *your* idea against *my* idea.

RIGHT AT EACH STAGE

It may be argued that in the end there has to be evaluation of an idea. At some stage there has to be rigorous scrutiny to tell whether the idea is safe, whether it will work, whether it will offer the promised benefits. It may be said that surely this is the right place for dialectic. I am not even sure that is true. I do not see why a joint evaluation (or even an independent evaluation) should not be even better. For the moment, however, let me say that I would have less objection to the argument mode at this stage.

The danger is that we actually believe that argument is a way of creating, designing and building up an idea. This is quite simply nonsense. If the argument mode is the only mode available in normal conflict situations then it is no wonder that there is so little creative design.

By definition the argument mode insists that you are right at each stage. This means that you are logically consistent and do not contradict yourself or the facts. You are also required to base each step on some evidence. Speculation and feeling are rigidly eschewed.

Now we do know that in the creative process there are provocations that are meant as provocations, not as truths (and are logically justified in the patterning system of perception). There are also half-truths, suggestions, hints of benefit. Not one of these could stand up to a logical attack and demand for justification. But they do not have to. They take their place in the self-organizing soup of creativity from which comes the final idea. It is this final idea that can then be made to justify itself logically.

It is a very old-fashioned notion to believe that an idea has to be right at each stage for the final idea to be right. This shows a complete lack of understanding of perception and patterning systems.

NEGATIVITY

One of the main purposes of the argument mode is to be negative. This has two aims. The first is to throw out statements or ideas which are incorrect or unjustified. The other, perhaps more important, aim is to make people think carefully about what they are going to say because it is liable to attack. In practice there is a simple way around this in conflict thinking. There are a large number of very convenient words which are, at the same time, broad, vague and value laden. They can be applied almost everywhere and they are immune from attack. They include such words as rights, freedom, oppression, justice, humanity, suffering. It can never be wrong to use them and in their wake they can carry forward any manner of argument. I shall come to them again later. Much could be said to depend on the intentions of those having the argument. Since conflict arguments are not carried out in an amicable frame of mind then it is obvious that the players are not going to stick nicely to the proper rules of argument.

We are then left with the sheer negativity of the idiom. Who gets to pick out the good points in the argument of the other side? Obviously this cannot be left to the combatants. This is an obvious role for the third party which will be suggested later in this book as part of the 'triangular idiom' of conflict thinking.

The negativity of the behavior engenders a negativity of mood that can itself limit perceptions, as I suggested in a preceding section. When in a negative mood we may simply be incapable of having constructive thoughts. In addition the negative mood of argument can create a negative mood of behavior and the way each participant treats the others. Winning or losing points becomes a conflict in itself and not just a discussion about a conflict. It is something of an absurdity to try to solve one conflict with another one.

It is theoretically possible to have very civilized arguments when both parties are highly sophisticated and know the rules of the game. Experience in the courts of law suggests, however, that even very experienced and sophisticated antagonists soon get carried away by the idiom of winning and losing and forget about argument as exploration. A lawyer sees it as his duty to hammer on a weak point and to try to distract attention away from a stronger point in the opponent's case.

At this point I am not making a case for creativity. I am making a case for what is constructive — for where achievement comes from building something up rather than attacking it. The construction may be pretty ordinary, with no flourish of creativity, but even that ordinary constructiveness is not likely to emerge from the negativity of the argument mode.

BEING RIGHT

If negativity is the main fighting tool of the argument mode then being right is the main achievement point. Being right is a mixture of proving immune from attack and having a coherent argument which is tidily organized. The feeling may also come from having carried through a devastating attack. Just how important is being right?

There is a spectrum of 'being right' that ranges from the complicated calculations needed to land a man on the exact spot on the moon to grandmother's guess that it will rain later in the afternoon. 'Being right' is a sort of paradise that bestows all manner of goodies once you get there: wisdom, character, admirableness, competence, etc.

We need to put a high value on our doctors being right and our airline pilots being right. There is a real test of their rightness. That sort of rightness is very different from the rightness of a politician or one side in a dispute.

Any reasonably intelligent person can construct a coherent argument to support his or her point of view — whatever that may be. That is what we call the 'intelligence trap'. An intelligent person uses thinking to support a point of view rather than to explore other points of view — and is thereby trapped by the excellence of the support that is assembled.

Being right is not too difficult. You choose your perceptions, you select your information, you leave out what does not suit you, you drag in some general-purpose value words, you throw in a sneer or two about the opposition and you are a fine fellow who has made a fine speech. Though totally irrelevant from an information point of view, the sneer is a very fine conflict tool because it achieves its effect without having to say anything. In a way it is a pure essence of negativity.

THE RULES OF THE GAME

Once you are within the game you have to play by the rules. That is a basic point I shall keep coming back to again and again in this book. That is why there is a point in setting up structures and systems of thinking (other than argument). The players learn to play to the rules and then find themselves thinking in a different way.

If you take a group of people full of good will and sweet reason and then ask them to play the adversarial or argument game, it is hardly surprising that the outcome is of the conflict type. There are positions to be defended, victories to be gained and defeats to be inflicted. Why should we expect it to be anything different?

So the goodwill of those taking part is no protection against the idiom of the argument mode.

THE GENERAL PURPOSES OF ARGUMENT

We use argument a great deal. So what do we use it for?

1. To prove that someone is wrong. To prove that one thing does not follow from another. To prove that he contradicts himself. To prove that he is inconsistent. And in general to point out all the other possible sources of error: partialism, magnitude effect and all the other errors I have mentioned elsewhere in my books.

2. To show someone up to be stupid or ignorant: and therefore all he or she says is quite worthless. To show someone up to be inconsiderate, callous or a bully: and hence a detestable person. To show someone up to be dishonest, shifty and unreliable. In all cases it follows that their ideas and logic can be no better than their persona.

3. To make an impression on others as in the United Nations, parliament, a jury or a T.V. audience.

4. To set the emotional mood that will then become part of the negotiating scene. This mood setting may be tough, strong, bullying or obdurate. This is a real contribution to the argument and affects the sort of ideas that can be used, as I mentioned in an earlier section.

5. To cast doubt on the certainty of a particular interpretation (for instance in court) and to suggest the possibility of alternative explanations. This is the closest argument ever gets to creativity.

6. To force an *exploration* of a matter. To demonstrate your view and to open up the other view. To push each view further (into the future) and deeper (into the value base). To show differences of opinion as to what is and also what may happen as a consequence of action. To show how both views may coexist under different circumstances. To flesh out and extend the whole matter.

7. To bring about an insight change of view. To help someone suddenly see something differently.

It is quite obvious that the most desired of all outcomes is the insight change of view (point 7). If this were common then it would be sufficient justification for the judgment mode. Unfortunately it is extremely rare. In any case, if it is insight that we want to bring about then the type of 'mapping' thinking that I shall be describing in the next section would be much more effective. Consider this simple example.

A person was complaining about a water shortage and how the taps were turned off without warning. She felt that proper notice should be given that the taps would be off between certain hours. The listener agreed that that would be helpful but wondered if people might then hoard water in bathtubs and basins and so actually consume more water. The complainer immediately saw the point because that was in fact exactly what she had done during a water shortage in Hong Kong many years before. In this case insight clicked in with a piece of personal experience.

It may also be felt that exploration (point 6) is the real purpose of argument. It may be a by-product but it is not the main purpose. If it were then it would be a discussion not an argument. An argument presupposes ready-made points treated with attack and defense. By definition, exploration is the eliciting of further points. Once again, if exploration is really the point of argument then we can go about it in a more direct and effective way with the type of thinking described in the next section. There is an alternative to argument.

CHAPTER 3

MAP-MAKING, THINKING AND THINK-2

To attack the argument idiom is only another example of argument thinking unless some alternative is offered. That alternative is 'design' thinking. This implies a constructive exploration of the situation with a view to designing an outcome. In some respects this is like making a map, showing the possible routes and eventually choosing a route. The map-making instruments described in this section are very simple and very basic. They are the ones that are used in the school program for the teaching of thinking. Eventually, map-making instruments may need to be much more sophisticated, but even these simple tools suffice to show the difference between argument and map-making.

An explorer might make a sketch of the new land around him by looking to the North and drawing what he sees; then looking to the East; then to the South and finally to the West. At the end he will have a simple map of the terrain. North, South, East and West are merely convenient directions in which to focus his attention. He is able to tackle the map piece by piece.

We can apply a very similar process to thinking.

For months a businessman had been negotiating with a major oil company over some deal. There were exchanges of letters and visits by lawyers and the usual apparatus of a lengthy negotiation. One day the businessman was in a group that was taught the P.M.I.* lesson. This is the first of the thinking lessons that I designed many years ago for the direct teaching of thinking in schools. The P.M.I. is practiced as a tool on a variety of situations so that skill is built up in the use of the tool that can then be applied to new situations. This is one way around the major problem of transferring thinking skills from one situation to another.

The P.M.I. asks the thinker to look first in the Plus direction (all the good points). Then in the Minus direction (all the bad points). Finally in the

*Note that the P.M.I. and other tools mentioned here are proprietary educational material published by Pergamon Press Ltd.

Interesting direction (all the interesting things that are worthy of comment but may be neither good nor bad). The discipline has to be adhered to: one thing at a time. So the thinker makes a thorough job of looking for the Plus points, the Minus points and the Interesting points. At the end there is a simple map. The thinker (or thinkers) now look at the map and make their decisions.

The purpose of the P.M.I. is, of course, to counteract the natural tendency to take a view based on emotion and then to use thinking *only to back up* that view — as in the 'intelligence trap' I mentioned before.

So the P.M.I. forces a scan or the making of a simple map.

So at his next meeting the businessman explained the P.M.I. process and the group agreed to try it out. He told me that the matter which had been going on for months was now solved in about twenty minutes.

This is not surprising. Instead of each side thinking 'against' the other as in the usual argument method, both sides were now making a map. That was the first stage and they tried to make a good map as any map maker would. Once the map had been made then the thoughts which had been thought could not be unthought. It was now a question of reacting to the map according to needs, values and objectives.

On another occasion a mother had decided to move from California to Arizona. This decision had been prepared and argued with her two sons over two years. She and her sons also attended a class where the P.M.I. lesson was being taught. When they got home they decided to 'do a P.M.I.' on the planned move. In half an hour the mother had decided not to move to Arizona after all.

The head of a major supermarket chain decided to use the P.M.I. (and some of the other tools) in his annual wage negotiating round. He told me that it was all over much more quickly and much more simply than it had ever been before.

To anyone who attends such meetings there is a huge difference between this structured type of exploration and the usual argument method. It is not unlike the Japanese exploration idiom I mentioned in the last section: both sides are doing their best to *explore and map make.*

At a demonstration class in a Sydney school I asked the 30 boys (aged about ten years old) if they would each like five dollars each week for coming to school. All 30 of them thought it a wonderful idea and gave their reasons: buying sweets, comics, etc. I then explained the P.M.I. scanning tool in a brief manner. I asked them to apply the P.M.I. to the five-dollar-a-week suggestion. This they then did in groups of five. After about four minutes of discussion they reported back to me. The Plus points were much the same as before. There were, however, now some Minus points (bigger boys might take the money, less money for teachers, etc.) and some Interesting points (would parents still give them pocket money?). At the end of this simple exercise I put the question again. This time 29 out of 30 of the boys had completely reversed their view and thought the five dollars a week would be a bad idea.

The important point with this story is that a simple scanning tool used by the thinkers themselves led to a reversal of a decision and a reversal against their normal instincts. I do want to emphasize that this was exactly the opposite of an argument. I did not point out the problems or difficulties or ask them to justify their choice. I just left it to them to make a map and then to use it.

It all sounds very simple — and it is. But it is also very powerful.

TEACHING THINKING IN SCHOOLS

The P.M.I. is just the first one of the 60 lessons that form part of the Co.R.T. Program for the direct teaching of thinking as a skill in schools. Co.R.T. stands for Cognitive Research Trust, and there are more than 13 years experience with the lessons. They are designed to be robust and practical and usable by teachers of varying ability with youngsters (and adults) of differing ages and intelligence. Although it is all very simple at the end, the design of the method and materials is directly based on considerations of the nature of perceptual thinking (as I described in the previous section) and also on the need to have transferable tools.

This program of mine now seems to be the most widely used in the world for the direct teaching of thinking in schools — a subject area that is rapidly growing in importance. In Venezuela every schoolchild, by law, spends two hours a week on thinking skills. There is quite widespread use in Canada and growing use in the U.S.A. The method is used in the U.K., Ireland, Australia and New Zealand in different schools. I have set up pilot projects in Bulgaria, Malaysia and Malta and have invitations to set up further projects. The preliminary results from Bulgaria show statistically significant increases in intelligence and other measured attributes. Results from Canada, Australia and the U.S.A. also show measurable effects.

I mention these things as a matter of interest and to put the P.M.I. and the other tools into perspective. They are not part of some new gimmick. They have been tried over many years in many different conditions (from the most elite school in Canada to the jungle of Eastern Venezuela). They do work.

UNBUNDLING THINKING

There was a time when I.B.M. used to sell hardware and software and perhaps even service contracts all together. Then there came the great 'unbundling'. Each item came to be treated separately.

In general, we try to do too much at once with our thinking. We get cluttered and confused. We end up by doing just one thing: carrying through the negative attack of the argument method.

P.M.I. is one tool. C.&S. (Consequence and Sequel) is another. It becomes a matter of doing one thing at a time and doing it well. For any occasion we can pick and choose the tools that are needed. If we are looking at the short- and long-term consequences of an action, then that is what we do.

So how does it all come together at the end? It comes together as a map.

COLOR PRINTING

At one time I was tempted to call this 'mosaic' thinking because in the end each separate piece comes together to give the whole. Color printing is probably a better analogy.

The color separations are made. Then each color is printed on separately. From the overlap of the colors the full four-color picture is formed and might be a high-class reproduction of a Rubens. A similar process takes place with color photography.

In an exactly similar way, each of the Co.R.T. thinking tools covers the area with one 'color'. In the end all the colors come together to give the full map.

This idiom of color printing, which is done in separate stages and builds up to a full-color picture in the end, is particularly applicable to the concept of the 'six thinking hats' which I shall be mentioning later in this book (and which is the basis of another book).

CARPENTER'S TOOLS

There are times when the analogy of a carpenter's tools might also be appropriate. A carpenter learns when to use hammer, chisel or plane and acquires skill in the use of each. In the making of a particular piece of furniture the carpenter may go through a fine sequence of tools — as required. It can be exactly the same with the Co.R.T. thinking tools.

Consider the richness of a choice from amongst a wide number of thinking tools as compared with the very restricted thinking involved only in proving someone to be wrong — as in argument. It is only too obvious which type of thinking will give the better map.

With the map-making approach we may be looking at priorities, objectives, values, other people's views, types of outcome and many other matters.

THINKING AS A TWO-STAGE PROCESS

It has been implicit all along that the map-making style of thinking is a two-stage process:

1st. Make the map.
2nd. Use the map.

Instead of someone just thinking about something or arguing with someone there is a thinking task (which may be an A.P.C. — looking for Alternatives, Possibilities and Choices). The thinker carries out that task then he, or she, reacts to what has been brought forth: reacts to what is now on the map.

THINK-2

Many years ago in a book of mine called 'Practical Thinking' (still published by Penguin Books Ltd., London) I coined the term 'Think-2'. I never did much about it. The purpose of this term was to contrast this exploratory or map-making type of thinking with the more usual argument (truth/falsity) type of thinking which, by definition, was Think-1.

It also works out that 'Think-2' can symbolize a two-stage thinking process: draw the map and use the map. The whole point is that drawing the map is a neutral process. It is quite different from the conflict type of thinking to be found in argument.

SUBJECTIVE MAPS

But would a person ever draw an honest map which was to that person's disadvantage? I doubt very much whether a thief can be expected to put his guilt down on the map. Short of that the map tends to be honest because it is always subjective. The map is always drawn from each thinker's point of view.

In a P.M.I. exercise on the desirability of painting all cars yellow (from the safety and visibility point of view), one boy put down as a Plus point that such cars would tend to be kept cleaner. Another boy put down exactly the same point as a Minus point: because he would have to clean his Dad's car more often. Both were, of course, correct.

Different subjective maps can be compared and contrasted. The points of similarity and the points of difference become quite obvious. If a common map is to be made then something can be put down as having both Plus value and Minus value at the same time (in spite of problems with contradiction).

In the map-making stage no positions are taken in such a way as to exclude another position. In contradiction of the principle of contradiction two mutually exclusive positions can exist simultaneously. That is part of the richness of the map.

THINK-2 AND CONFLICT THINKING

Throughout this section I have been suggesting a map-making type of thinking as an alternative to argument and clash. I have suggested exploration instead of attempting to design ideas with a hatchet.

It must be obvious that I feel very strongly that this map-making type of thinking would have an important role to play in conflict resolution. Why should we be restricted to the argument mode?

It might be said that two parties hot for argument would not want to be diverted by map-making exercises of the sort suggested here. In practice this does not seem to be the case because both parties usually feel that their own case is so good that a map will only clarify the merits of the case. There will always be extreme cases where the combatants are enjoying the conflict for its own sake and are not genuinely interested in any resolution. That is usually a temporary phase.

There does not have to be agreement between the parties. One party can, on its own, start to carry out these formal map-making exercises: a P.M.I. can be inserted at one point, an A.P.C. at another. The other party will be drawn into the exercise as otherwise the only map around will have been drawn by the opponent.

THIRD PARTY ROLE

Later in the book I shall be discussing in much more detail the third party role in conflict thinking. For a number of reasons I believe it to be an essential role

— and not just as a go-between. The nature of conflict thinking makes a third party thinking point imperative. That is how 'triangular thinking' comes about. Without third party involvement conflict thinking remains one-dimensional. There can be no real design element. At best there is only a compromise effect which is far short of good design.

I shall be writing about this important third party role later. At this point I mention it because the third party is in an ideal position to request map-making exercises from time to time. At worst the parties can respond with churlishness or incompetence, both of which are obviously unattractive stances. As before, failure to help in making a map simply means that one will be made on your behalf — by the third party if necessary. You would only be left with the power of modification, for denial would have no function. To claim that a geographer's map is incorrect is meaningless unless you actually point out where it is incorrect. At that instant you are providing your version of the map. In practice things do work out this way.

The sort of third party I have in mind is neither a neutral chairman nor a judge. He is someone who takes an active part in the process of thinking and of design.

ROLE PLAYING

If you role play being a thinker you will become a thinker.

This seems an outrageous claim but it seems to be true. If you go through the motions of being a thinker you will indeed find yourself thinking. It is not really so surprising. If you formally set yourself to do a P.M.I. then the carrying out of it is quite simple. In time it becomes a habit. In time you become the thinker you have tried to be.

At this point it is worth mentioning why the tools have such artificial sounding names as P.M.I., C.&S. or A.P.C. The reason is simple. Exhortation has no permanent value, no tool value and no role-playing value. You can exhort someone to have a balanced view of a matter and that person will try to do so — for the time being. Years of training might have a more permanent effect. But the P.M.I. can be learned in a few minutes and used thereafter as a deliberate tool. To be distinct and deliberate such a tool must have an identity. Just as the mind is filled with descriptive concepts (table, chair, meal, etc.) so we need to feed into consciousness some 'operator concepts'. So the P.M.I. lodges in the mind as a strange new animal. It has an identity.

We have found that when teachers have tried to teach the same matters but refused to use the 'jargon' the effect is too weak. Pupils may go through the exercise but there is no permanence, no referral value and above all, no transfer value. To have a tool you have to create a tool.

ROLE REVERSAL

This is a different type of role playing. In conflict situations each side is much concerned with its own point of view. The opposing point of view is only examined as a commander might examine opposing defenses: for weaknesses. Yet an understanding of the other point of view is a most useful step in conflict resolution.

Role reversal, in which each side puts itself into the opposing position, is an established part of conflict resolution. In the Co.R.T. set of map-making tools there are three specific operators which cover this point.

A.D.I.: this stands for areas of Agreement, Disagreement and Irrelevance. The parties set out to make a 'map' showing those areas about which there is agreement. Those areas where the disagreement is really lodged. And those areas which may keep coming into the conflict but which can be judged to be irrelevant. It is often surprising how small the areas of disagreement can be once the 'argument mode' has been exchanged for the 'map mode'.

E.B.S.: this stands for Examine Both Sides. It is traditional role reversal in which each side has to spell out — honestly and fully — the case for the other side.

O.P.V.: this stands for Other People's Views. This is a more general-purpose tool. Thinking situations usually involve many more parties than the person doing the thinking. The O.P.V. exercise consists of identifying these other parties and then looking at the world from the point of view of each of these parties. It is less detailed than the E.B.S. but much wider in scope, since it includes parties not taking part in the dispute but likely to be affected by it.

THE USE OF THE MAPPING TOOLS

My role in this section has been to show Think-2 or mapping thinking as an alternative to the argument method. Having spent the preceding section attacking the argument method, I had an obligation to suggest an alternative. I have presented the mapping method and the Co.R.T. mapping tools in a very brief manner. The method needs to be learned formally and developed as a skill. There are materials available for that purpose*. I have

*Available from Pergamon Press Ltd.

done no more than indicate how mapping thinking works — in an effort to contrast it with argument. This type of thinking is only one of the aspects of conflict thinking that I shall be dealing with in this book. It would, however, have been typical of the sterility of the critical method to attack 'argument' and to put nothing in its place.

THE PURPOSE OF A MAP

A girl of 13 was carrying out a P.M.I. exercise. She happened to be doing it on her own in a written form (the usual form is a group discussion). This is what she said at the end:

> At first I thought it was all rather silly because I knew very well what I thought about the subject. I did not need a P.M.I. to tell me. Then I started putting things down under P and then under M and finally under I. When I had finished I found to my surprise that my own mind had been totally changed by what I, myself, had put down on the paper.

This is a very clear illustration of what is meant by the 'insight' purpose of exploration. By having a clearer map of her *own thoughts* the thinker had come to a different conclusion — without any outside help. It also illustrates the purpose of a thinking 'tool' which the thinker uses for herself or himself. And all this achieved with an extremely simple scanning tool.

CHAPTER 4

FIGHT, NEGOTIATE, PROBLEM-SOLVE OR DESIGN?

It is very important to be clear about the idiom of conflict thinking. What is the action: fight, negotiate, problem-solve or design?

I am ready to accept that there are a few occasions when a particular situation calls for one — and only one — of these four alternatives. There may indeed be a specific problem that has to be solved: for example the pollution of a lake. At other times there may be a specific negotiating situation: for example the complex factors affecting a wage settlement. I want to leave aside these very specific examples in order to take a broad look at conflict thinking.

With some exceptions just mentioned, we can *choose* to look at any conflict situation with our own preferred idiom.

We can choose to treat all conflicts as fights. This refers both to the conflict itself (which may be a real fight) and also to the thinking that is taking place to resolve the conflict. Here I am concerned with that thinking. If a conflict is a fight does the thinking about it also have to be a fight? It seems obvious and natural that it should — but there is no good reason at all why it has to be so (except perhaps the continuity we shall meet later).

The 'fight' idiom involves all the battle jargon. There are tactics and strategy. There are offensive positions and defensive positions and fall-back positions. There is gaining ground and losing ground. There are weak points to be exposed. This may be the idiom of the courtroom, where winning or losing a case is the purpose with justice as an expected by-product.

This 'fight' idiom has always been the usual conflict idiom. This could be because the parties always find themselves in that mood. I suspect it is because we have so admired, and always used, the argument clash that the parties are permanently kept in the fight mood whether they like it or not. There is a self-fulfilling prophecy. The idioms and language we use create the mood which then fosters the idiom and language. We expect to 'fight' and we hold ourselves in an antagonistic stance. There may be times when leaders and negotiators feel it to be their duty to reflect the mood of those who are having to do the front-line fighting. It might seem slightly indecent for negotiators to be friendly in the comfort of an air-conditioned meeting room (with food and drink) whilst front-line troops are risking their lives in appalling conditions.

Nevertheless we do have to ask the question: is the 'fight' idiom, as applied to conflict thinking, the best way of getting a resolution of the conflict? My own answer is that it is certainly not. Nor can I see any logical reason for expecting that it should have a creative effect. It is time we accepted this for the *nonsense* it is.

There is no reason why the mode of the conflict itself should be extended into the thinking about the conflict.

NEGOTIATE

Surely this is the right mood? I am not sure that it is. Negotiation suggests a compromise. It suggests a position that is somewhere between the two existing positions. In the lengthy and expensive metalworkers' strike in Germany in 1984 the final compromise was a working week of 38½ hours. The unions had wanted a 35-hour week as a reduction from the current 40-hour week. Often physical boundaries are drawn.

There is a weakness about all this. From a thinking point of view we are restricting ourselves to what already exists. It is the same objection that I have to the argument method. With argument we spend our time attacking existing ideas rather than designing new ones. With negotiation we work within the boundaries that exist rather than design new ones.

There is also something weak about the role of a negotiator. He is supposed to be a humble servant of the warring parties. He has to scuttle to and fro to carry communications they refuse to direct to each other. He must try to keep them all happy. He is a sort of lubricant. In later sections I shall acknowledge this particular third party role and indicate why I think it is inadequate.

The negotiating idiom is superior to the fight idiom because at least it is different from the idiom of the conflict itself. There is, however, the danger of *appeasement*. Negotiation involves value trading. There is nothing wrong with that but if the idiom is well established then the combatants feed in superfluous demands simply as trading material.

Bargaining is always an improvement on arguing but I would see negotiation very much as a last resort. I would regard negotiation as inferior to both problem-solving and to design.

Negotiations have usually been handled by lawyers as an extension of their arguing role. There is the same underlying idiom: let us play around with what is rather than design something new.

A client has ordered a sculpture for the forecourt of the corporate headquarters in Philadelphia (which city has sensibly decided that a fraction of the cost of any new building must be spent on an associated work of art). The sculptor comes along with two alternative models.

> 'Which one do you prefer?'
> 'I do not really like either.'
> 'Those are the only two choices. The opening is on May 5th, and everything is set. The sculptures have to be in place by then. Think of all the money you will lose otherwise. Besides, this company has got where it is by doing things as planned — opening on time.'
> 'I am still not happy.'
> 'Let's talk about it. What don't you like? Perhaps we can make you happier. For example those angular pieces that are all the fashion now. They don't last. They look great in a photograph in the first annual report. But after some months they look like a piece of junk. Look at these nice curves. Curves last.'
> 'Those leave me cold.'
> 'So react to them intellectually. It's a good price. My name is good. Trust me. After all who knows best, me or you?'
> 'Maybe if we brought the price down a bit I could regard them as temporary and then we can replace them some years hence.'
> 'We can talk about that. You'll find everyone wants to keep them.'
> 'I quite like this curly bit here on this one. But I prefer that grey-bronze color of the other one — it looks powerful. That's the sort of image we want to project. And that curly bit suggests venture and enterprise.'
> 'I tell you what. I'll go ahead with this one but we'll paint it the grey-bronze that you liked on this other one.'
> 'Can you do that?'
> 'It's not perfect but it's not a perfect world. It is workable. And you'll have the piece on time.'
> 'And we shall talk about the price . . .'

I know this is an unfair piece but it does serve to give that compromise flavor of negotiation that is so unsatisfactory.

Quite simply, negotiation as an idiom is not good enough in conflict thinking.

PROBLEM SOLVING

You want to do something? So, that is a problem. So you solve the problem.

'Problem solving' as a general purpose idiom has become very popular in the U.S.A. in business, in government, in academic circles and in personal life. There are all sorts of books on how to solve the problems of day-to-day competition and personal fulfillment.

I am not happy with this problem-solving idiom either.

A doctor is called to see a woman who looks ill, has a pain in the chest and is breathing rapidly. His first 'problem' is to find out what is the matter: to diagnose the trouble. He carries out a physical examination which suggests pneumonia. The woman is rushed to hospital where an X-ray supports the diagnosis. The next problem might be to identify the particular bug which is causing the infection. At this point a further practical problem arises. Identifying the bug could take time and the woman is very ill. So the doctor prescribes a broad spectrum antibiotic whilst an attempt is made to identify the infecting agent.

Here we can see a succession of problems and their solution. There is the overall problem of the infecting agent which has caused pneumonia. If we can get rid of that 'cause' we can cure the illness and restore health. This is a very common type of problem: this thing has gone wrong, can we put it right.

This type of problem has been called a 'deviation' from the normal. Health is normal, sickness is a deviation, remove the sickness. The problem-solving mode is very straightforward: identify the cause and remove it. For a long time this was an immensely successful idiom in medicine. Tuberculosis, which used to be 'the captain of the men of death' is now insignificant in developed countries. Drugs have been found to fight (and remove) the infecting cause.

Analyze the problem, find the cause, put it right is a simple and attractive idiom. It makes sense and it is action oriented. Unfortunately it is inadequate. As with the argument mode there is exactly the same danger of our veneration of an inadequate idiom: we feel it to be sufficient when it is not.

Why is this remove-cause idiom inadequate? For a number of reasons. In a complex interactive situation we may never be able to isolate one cause since there are a large number of interacting factors. This is why progress in medicine suddenly slowed down when the simpler remove-cause diseases had been dealt with and medicine had to cope with more complex behavior like high blood pressure, heart disease and cancer.

In conflict situations, as in medicine, there is a danger in fastening on to a particular cause because it is easy to identify, ignoring the rest of the

39

situation, and staking everything on removing that cause. Complex systems simply do not work that way — even when our sense of tidiness would want them to.

We may never be able to find a cause. Or, we may never be able to prove that a particular suspect really is the cause. In medicine we can do some experiments. In conflict situations we largely have to rely on experience and speculation.

Let us suppose that we do identify the cause. But we cannot remove it. What do we do then? Do we wring our hands and call it an insoluble problem — as often happens in conflict situations?

There is also the notion that once the cause is removed then the problem is solved and all will be well. Kill the pneumococcus bug that causes pneumonia and the patient is cured. We often suppose that if a dictator is removed then democracy will burst into bloom — the cause of the problem has been removed. What we need to note is that whilst the cause was in action the effects and adjustments were so widespread that it may no longer simply be a matter of problem solving 'by removing the cause of the problem'.

So there is a serious limitation to the simplistic problem solving that focuses on identifying the cause and removing it.

It should be noted carefully that with problem solving we always know *where we want to end up*. This is the case with the deviation type of problem. We know where we are and what is normal. Remove the deviation and we shall be back to normal. Applied to conflict thinking this suggests that if only we can get rid of the conflict then things will be back to what they were before. This is not usually the case, as I suggested earlier.

We come now to the second type of problem. Here we know exactly where we want to go — but have to find a way of getting there. We saw several of this type of problem with the doctor and the pneumonia patient: the need to make a diagnosis; the need to confirm the diagnosis; the need to give immediate treatment; the need to identify the agent. With both a plan and a problem we know where we want to get. With the plan we know how, with the problem we do not yet know how. That is where problem solving comes in.

Just as the cause-removal type of problem solving could be applied to conflict thinking, so too can the how-to-get-there variety of problem solving. All we need to do is to define where we want to be and then to devise the best means of getting there. I want to get to New York on Friday: how do I get there? I want to stop missile attacks on the tankers: how do I do that?

Here we come to a very important point about problem solving. It is this.

How precise does our definition of the destination have to be?

'I want to get to New York by 9pm this Friday evening' is a precise requirement.

'I want to do some traveling' is very broad and vague.

If we allow the definition to be very broad and vague then there is little point in talking about a 'problem'. We might just as well talk about a want or intention or wish. So unless we are going to play semantic games we should keep the term 'problem solve' to situations where we have a fairly precise definition of where we want to get to. In practice this is very important because very broad problem definition is really just a 'design wish'. The types of thinking required for problem solving and for design are not the same. The danger of allowing problem definitions to be too broad is that we end up applying problem-solving techniques when really we should be using design techniques.

Problem solving certainly does have a place in conflict thinking. The main limitation is that we may put much too definite a view on what we believe the solution should be before we have really done our thinking about the matter. As soon as we say 'this is the problem' we have defined the sort of solution we expect. I have already commented about the limitation of the remove-cause idiom.

DESIGN

By the end of this book it will be no secret that my preference is for the design idiom. I shall come back to it again and again as the underlying mode of thinking in conflict situations.

With design we set out to design something. There is an output. There is something to be achieved.

It is not just a matter of removing a problem or effecting a compromise. There is a designed something which was not there before.

With design there is a sense of purpose and a sense of fit. Things are brought together or shaped in order to fulfill some purpose. It might be a boat or a house or a baby's shoe.

Argument, negotiation and problem analysis are always looking back at what is already there. Design is always looking forward at what might be created.

Design is much more towards the self-organizing and perceptual style of thinking than is analysis, which is concerned with reference and truth.

With design there may be provocations, false starts, concept leaps and an uneven development process. This is quite unlike the step-by-step, right-at-each-stage idiom of book-keeping.

In conflict thinking we need to *design outcomes*. I do not even like saying design 'solutions' because this implies that there is a problem.

A conflict is a situation which needs a design effort.

Even if we cannot find a cause or, after finding it, cannot remove it, we can always attempt to design an outcome.

What I am suggesting is that we really drop the word 'conflict'. Instead of treating conflict thinking as something very special because of the conflict element we say: 'this is a situation that needs design thinking to design an outcome'. The conflict element then comes in as one of the key design ingredients.

The merit of this approach is that we are no longer trapped into believing that thinking about conflicts must itself be conflict thinking. In the negotiating mode there is ever-present the idiom of two opposing sides (trading, bargaining, giving and taking). All that is gone when we shift to the design idiom.

Where, then, does the special 'conflict' character of the situation come in? It comes in at two stages. It comes in as an ingredient in that *information environment* stage which is so vital a part of all design. It comes in again in the 'fit' stage which is the whole purpose of design: to fit the purpose and to fit the client.

The mapping type of thinking described in the previous section is precisely the sort of factor feeding that is required in design. There has to be this environment of information (and feelings) in which the design starts to take shape. That sort of input could never come from argument. Nor could it come from just 'being around'. This might suffice for the long (lifetime) period available to an artist but in a deliberate design situation there has to be a way of creating the input of the situation: the design brief.

We come now to the matter of 'fit'.

When Ben Lexcen designed the novel keel for the Australian boat that took the America's Cup away from the New York Yacht Club, there had to be three sorts of fit. First there had to be a fit of 'competence'. This means complying with normal boat requirements (stress, sea-worthy, etc.) and also with the race regulations. This is just the baseline. An architect must design a stable and safe building. Then there was the fit of the special requirement. The boat had to be a little bit faster than anything else ever designed. That sort of design aim is admirable but quite out of place in conflict resolution, where reliability would take its place. Finally there had to be client fit. Ben Lexcen had to know that Alan Bond was sufficiently daring and unconventional to take a risk with the new design and to enjoy the notoriety.

The designer of an advertising campaign has to go through layers of 'fit'. The campaign must sell the goods. It must fit the image of the client corporation. It must fit the image of the advertising agency. It must fit the budget. It must fit the competitors' stance.

Design is all about fit.

Obviously 'fit' is important in a conflict situation since the designed outcome must be acceptable to the fighting parties and to other interested parties. Indeed, 'fit' is the *only* alternative to the victory/defeat idiom (where fit is not required).

Needless to say, creativity plays a very great part in the design idiom. But it is careful, concept creativity, not a scatter-gun approach of novelty for the sake of novelty. There is a lot of rubbish that goes by the name of creativity when it is no more than bizarre aberration. I shall be dealing with creativity in a later part of the book.

The main point about the design idiom is that it is open ended. We set out to achieve an outcome. At the beginning we do not know exactly what the outcome is going to be, though there is yet a strong sense of purpose. A mountaineer has a peak to climb but a dancer has energy which then calls forth the steps.

We think of designers of buildings, boats, cars, fabrics and clothes. Yet the design of ideas is just as much a design process. I suppose that all my life I have been a designer of ideas and concepts.

SUMMARY

With regard to conflict thinking, I believe we must start with the best. We must start with the design idiom because it offers the most. The next best would be the problem-solving idiom. Then would come the negotiating idiom which could always be regarded as a fall-back position (it is insufficiently creative for a lead position). If all else fails then we are back to the 'fight' idiom. But that is very different from starting with the 'fight' idiom and never getting anywhere else. Which is largely the way we handle conflict thinking at the moment. Because we are so infatuated with the nonsense of dialectic.

I am not supposing that the usual combatants or negotiators are suddenly going to blossom forth a design talent (though they might, given the right frame). That is where the third party of the triangular thinking idiom comes in again. But that third party comes in as a designer, not as a fetch-and-carry go-between.

PART II
WHY DO PEOPLE DISAGREE?

CHAPTER 5

WHY DO PEOPLE DISAGREE? BECAUSE THEY SEE THINGS DIFFERENTLY

A conflict implies that two people are operating in the same situation. This may not apply to all their activities but it certainly applies to their 'conflict' activities. Two boys shadow-boxing in adjoining rooms are not fighting each other.

The two parties in a conflict may indeed be in the same situation —except that it is not the same situation to each of them. A child has been knocked down by a car. That is the situation. But it is not the same situation to the mother of the child, the car driver, a witness and the policewoman.

So conflicts arise because people may have to interact in the same situation but they see the situation very differently.

In an earlier book ('Practical Thinking'), I facetiously put forward what I called 'de Bono's first law':

'Everyone is always right. No one is ever right.'

This means that within his or her own perceptions a person may be right but in terms of wider perceptions this is not so and in terms of absolute perceptions it may never be so.

There are a number of reasons why people may see the same situation differently. It is important to note them, as understanding such differences is an essential part of conflict resolution.

MOOD

Earlier in the book I mentioned the possible differences that changes in the chemical setting of the brain may have on the way we perceive things. If we are in a certain mood we may only be able to see things in a certain way.

There is the old story of the optimist who saw the glass as being half full of whiskey and the pessimist who stoutly maintained that it was half empty. This is funny enough because we can see the equivalence of the two points of view. Many conflict situations are almost as trivial but there is no way of showing the equivalence of the two ways of looking at the situation. This is an example of a place where the design need would come in.

What can we do about mood? We can take note of it and its effect on the available thinking. We can try to change mood deliberately by changes of setting and choices of people. We cannot directly use chemicals other than the traditional ones.

We might, however, seek to switch moods through deliberate role playing. In this case the role would be adopted deliberately and then the mood would grow to fit the *behavior* determined by the role. In a new book I am setting forth the concept of 'Six Thinking Hats'. The thinker metaphorically puts on one of these hats and then adopts the prescribed role. The hats are:

> White hat: neutral, information, facts and figures without comment.
> Black hat: negative logical, why it won't work, why it can't be done, why it does not fit experience patterns.
> Yellow hat: positive speculative, why it might work, what is hoped for, what the benefits might be.
> Red hat: pure emotion without any need to explain or justify, a plain surfacing of current feeling on the matter.
> Green hat: fertile, generative and creative, new ideas, suggestions and provocations.
> Blue hat: overview control hat to control the use of others and also to act as an organizer of the thinking itself.

These are artificial moods, but, like the masks in a Kabuki play, may lead the real moods to follow.

I do not intend to discuss here all the possible effects of mood on thinking and the practical matters that arise. For example there is the difficulty of an offer made in a good mood and then not followed through in a more sober mood.

There is occasionally a notion that to take advantage of a mood is somehow to trick someone (like making that person emotionally drunk and incapable). The bias is, of course, the opposite way. Any temporary respite from a mood of antagonism and suspicion is a genuine contribution to the constructive thinking that is needed.

CONTEXT

This is rather a broad word which covers the whole setting of the situation. For example, anyone who has ever visited Argentina knows that the

Malvinas (Falklands) figure quite largely in the national consciousness. From time to time there would be a piece in the paper about the islands. This is quite a different context from the one in which the Falklands figured in England (prior to the war).

In Russia there is a remarkably persistent consciousness of the Second World War. There is a consciousness of the twenty million killed, of war heroes and veterans and of commemorative days. This is quite unlike the war consciousness in the West. There is also a genuine media focus on the possibility of a Western attack.

Historical contexts are an obvious example of how the same situation can come to be seen differently. Northern Ireland is a classic example. If the miners in England had not succeeded in bringing down the government of Mr Heath would they have tried so hard to bring down the government of Mrs Thatcher?

Labour leaders who lived through the Great Depression of the Thirties might have a different context through which to view unemployment than younger people.

We can do no better than periodically ask the question: what is the context here? And the next question: how does the context differ for each party?

When a new advertising manager takes over in a large corporation the context in which he is going to view the work of the agencies is going to be very different from what it had been in the last days of his predecessor. Immediate history can be as important as remote and cultural history.

LIMITED VIEW

This is a mixture of myopia and parochialism. It means that someone simply *cannot* see beyond a certain distance. It is always rather hard for someone with a larger view to realize that 'limited view' is a real thing and not a matter of choice. A villager in Europe may be more impressed by his friend taking over the village store than by his brother taking over a large corporation in the U.S.A. It is not that the village store is more immediate but that there simply is no comprehension of a large corporation.

A person who can only see part of a triangle may describe what he sees as a line. A person with a wider view may describe an angle. A person with a full view describes the triangle. When they compare notes they cannot believe they are describing the same thing.

It is quite useless to say: 'Believe me when I tell you that if you could see more this is what you would see.' The perception of the person with a limited view is not open-ended. It is tied up and organized in terms of the limited view. There is no automatic readiness for extension. The person with a limited view does not feel he is enclosed behind a high wall and is itching to get a look over the top. The person is standing with his back to the wall and is looking inwards: neither aware of the wall nor the possibility of looking beyond it.

Whatever is going to make sense is going to have to make sense within the limited view.

LOCAL LOGIC

At first sight this may seem very similar to the 'limited view' concept but it is actually different, and different in an important way. With local logic a thinker may actually have a very wide view. Nevertheless a certain action is chosen because it makes sense in a very local scene. In other words there is 'local logic' behind the action or choice. Note that the emphasis is on 'logic' and not on 'view'.

Quite often this action which is locally logical is anything but logical in the wider sense.

A couple are stranded on a Pacific island when their yacht is shipwrecked. There is only one source of water on the island. The wife, who is a geologist, suspects that the water is heavily contaminated with lead. The husband, who is a doctor, knows that over time an accumulation of lead will cause the severe symptoms of lead poisoning and eventual madness. The local logic is that they must drink the water to survive. In long-term logic this water is poisonous. As happens in almost all such situations the local logic must win and they hope that time will rescue them from the disastrous effects of their actions.

Newspaper strikes are crippling because the money lost on sales and advertising can never be regained. Also there is a fear of a fall in circulation. So the local logic is to give in to manning and wage demands and to hope that in the future a rise in advertising rates will put things right.

A wife wants to spend the money whilst she is still young enough to enjoy it and she feels sure her husband will eventually make much more. He is not so sure and wants to make provisions for retirement. She threatens to leave him which suggests to him that having spent his money she could leave anyway. Her local logic is different from his.

There is a need in language for something which is highly beneficial in a local scene but at the same time damaging in a larger scene. When we refer to time we do have such expressions as 'short-term gains'. We need a word for something which is simultaneously good and bad depending on whether you look at local or larger logic.

LOGIC BUBBLE

When we disagree with what someone is doing we have two basic choices. We can regard that person as stupid/malevolent or we can regard that person as highly intelligent but acting in a bubble of perceptions and circumstances which dictate that action. In other words the person is acting highly intelligently within the logic bubble within which he finds himself. It is not logical behavior for a civil servant to innovate because the risks of innovation far outweigh the possible rewards. It does not make sense for a miner to defy his striking workmates because the risks to his family and future family life probably outweigh the benefits.

If you take the skin of a man, that contains his self. Imagine another layer of skin a few inches further out than the usual layer. Imagine the layer further out still. In the end we might imagine some bubble of space in which the person lives as if that space were part of himself. With the logic bubble concept it is not physical space but a set of circumstances and conditions.

There is considerable overlap between local logic and logic bubble and at times they may be identical. Logic bubble is always very personal and refers to a particular individual. Local logic is relative. The Federal Reserve in the U.S.A. may signal a higher interest rate to protect the U.S. money supply and to keep a curb on inflation. Although the U.S. economy is vast enough, that still counts as 'local logic' because there are the economies of the rest of the world and the debts of Latin American countries, all of which are affected by the higher interest rates.

Why is this being done? That question may have an answer in local logic.

Why is he doing this now? That question will have an answer in that person's logic bubble.

I first used the expression 'logic bubble' in my book 'Future Positive' (published by Penguin Books Ltd., London).

DIFFERENCES OF UNIVERSE

I mentioned differences of universe in the section where I dealt with the difference between the 'active' information universe of perception and the 'passive' information universe of processing. There was also the story of the three men, each of whom released a block of wood.

Universe differences are profoundly important and all great jumps in science come about through a shift in the understood universe of action (what Kuhn calls a paradigm shift).

Talking across universes is even worse than talking across languages. If you talk English to a Japanese who does not understand you then there is no communication — but there is a consciousness that there is no communication. With universes, if you are talking in one universe and the listener is listening in another universe there may be no real comprehension but the listener believes he or she is understanding. It is immensely frustrating. An astronaut trying to explain the weightlessness of space to someone who did not know about space travel would have a hard time even though words like 'float' are part of common experience. I sometimes have the same sort of feeling when I am talking to traditional philosophers.

The universe of economics is not the same as the universe of politics. The universe of technology is not the same as the universe of nation states. These are some of the universe switches that we fail to make in conflict thinking. A universe is a set of circumstances and rules of action which determine how things behave in that universe — the universe determines the law of 'nature' in that universe. As we saw, in the underwater universe wood floats upwards, on the surface of the earth it drops downward.

The other occasions when something similar to a switch of universe is called for include culture changes and ideology changes. By culture I do not just mean little gestures of politeness like not showing the soles of your feet to your companions in the Orient (when sitting drinking). I mean basic culture differences. For example, Western man finds it hard to comprehend that Japanese culture is a compartment one not an ego-linked one (at each moment a person fits into the setting or particular compartment in which that person is placed).

It must be said that it is rather difficult for a capitalist to understand Marxist ideology except as a caricature and a protest against capitalism. Similarly it must be equally difficult for a Marxist to understand the strange mixture of selfishness and caring that occurs in a capitalist society (whether or not this is an essential part of the system).

The important thing with understanding universe changes is to treat each universe as separate and complete in itself. Then it comes to have its own logic and its own consistency and it is possible to work within this. To make point-by-point comparisons and then to try to remember all these differences just adds up to confusion. Comparisons can be made of fundamental points in order to show up the differences. Then the new universe is understood around these fundamental points. For example, the group basis for Japanese culture is a key point.

A union executive is working in a different universe from a corporate executive. A corporate executive would like to get the credit for an initiative and is prepared to take the blame: he needs to be noticed to get promoted. A union executive would be willing to forego the credit and the risk of blame because progress depends on not being blamed and on working as part of a team.

Theoretically a universe change is much more profound than a system change. After all, there may be several systems within the same universe. In practical terms there is a spectrum which runs from basic universe changes to system differences.

To understand behavior, values and what may happen next, all actions have to be referred to the universe in which they are taking place.

INFORMATION

You know that the Foreign Minister sitting across the table from you is about to be replaced at the end of the month. No one else at the table knows it yet. You are clearly in a different position from the others at the table.

The Rothschilds signaling (by carrier pigeon) of the results of the battle of Waterloo, before anyone else, put their friends in a position to make a lot of money.

Two people bid for an attractive painting at an auction. One of them just likes the painting. The other is advised by an art expert friend who says that the painting could be very valuable.

It is easy enough to find examples where two people are apparently in the same situation but where each has different information. Clearly they are not in the same situation.

We could go into whether the information is true or reliable; whether it is fact or just speculation; whether it will be available to all soon or never. Later in the book we shall look at the place of secrecy in conflict thinking. Should the parties share the information in order to align more closely the situations in which they find themselves or should they maintain secrecy to maximize advantage?

What happens if you know that he knows that you know that he knows that you cannot say what you know? Such are the reflecting mirrors of classical diplomacy. Do they create value or unnecessary complexity?

If you suddenly learned that a decision had been made to locate an airport near to the house you had just agreed to sell, would you tell the prospective purchaser or reckon it to be his business to find out? That is the sort of advantage that is claimed for diplomacy that is less than completely open.

But what if you were a seller the second time around to the same buyer. Would you be trusted? Perhaps the 'local logic' of the first situation ends up by backfiring.

Such a difference of information is one of the major sources of a difference of perception and since it is technically one of the easiest types of difference to be put right, serious thought needs to be given to the virtues of secrecy. Obviously there are limits of confidentiality but the key question is whether a party should share as much information as possible — or as little as possible.

It is likely that anyone who favors a mapping and design approach to conflict thinking must favor disclosure, whereas anyone who favors the dialectic argument and conflict mode must favor secrecy.

Be sure, however, that if there is nothing worthwhile to hide then secrecy will earn the appropriate mistrust without providing any benefits — except perhaps bluff.

PART OF THE PICTURE

Television camera crews have a job to do so they become notorious for picking on those moments of action that make good television but give a distorted view of what is going on: the single punch-up in an orderly crowd. A head bloodied by a flying stone fills the T.V. screen as if typical of the whole bloody scene. Interest is the name of the game and a bloodied head is certainly more interesting than 99 unbloodied ones.

Two economists are arguing as to whether a particular country is amongst the more highly taxed countries in the world. One says it is: the other that it is not. It turns out that the total tax take as a percentage of the G.N.P. is quite low because consumer taxes are low. Personal tax rates, however, accelerate sharply so higher income brackets are indeed heavily taxed. So both are right. It depends on what you are looking at.

Both parties may see the whole picture but each then chooses to put the emphasis and importance on one particular aspect. In a wage demand emphasis may be placed on the absolute low level of wages; on the failure of wages to keep pace with the cost of living; on the higher wages enjoyed by some other groups; on working conditions; on promises that could be interpreted favorably.

Much of the ammunition for conflict thinking arises from this deliberate choice of part of the picture.

Disarmament talks are well known for their shifting emphases. Is it warheads or missiles? Is it where they are stationed or who has fire control? Should these other missiles be counted in? Does the accuracy matter? Does the age matter?

It is curious that we so easily accept the spurious arguments of selected emphasis. Do we really expect that to be worthwhile something has to be perfect? We seem compelled to answer every chosen attack. Could we not answer:

'Yes, that is true enough. But in perspective it is a minor matter.'

It is probable that criticism of this sort is welcomed as part of the political process and part of the conscience of society that urges it towards improvement.

'If there is one starving family, that is one too many.'

Whilst it is easy to dispel ignorance by making information available, it is very hard to shift an emphasis which has been chosen to serve a purpose. So people see things differently because they choose so to do. This is different from those other cases where they have no choice.

EXPERIENCE

Experience is personal information and it makes the same contribution to different visions. A person with experience will not over-react to an ultimatum: a novice might well do so. A person who knows the other negotiator will accept an amount of brusqueness as part of the ritual: a novice might be upset by it.

As we shall see later in the section on creativity, experience can be both a great aid and also a trap. It is an aid to recognition and interpretation of what is going on. It is a trap when it restricts us to cliché solutions. The more experience we have the more difficult it is to be fresh and original. But where an experienced person succeeds in being creative then that person is doubly effective: the patterns of experience are available with which to put the creativity into action.

Earlier in this section I mentioned how the experience of the antagonists may form the context in which the conflict thinking takes place.

PREDICTION

This is a mixture of experience and information and it is vital in conflict thinking. How will things turn out? What will happen if I concede here? What will happen if we agree on this? How will this agreement be received back home? What will happen if we hold out? All the action is going to take place in the future, which stretches from the very next moment to possibly hundreds of years ahead.

A skilled lawyer will see that a certain clause may provide an escape loophole later or that another clause will be unenforceable. A further clause is so badly phrased that 'a coach and horses might be driven through'. Then there are clauses which it is foreseen will cause endless trouble and are best omitted.

Wisdom is usually taken as the key to prediction. It is wisdom that is supposed to predict how human beings will behave. Human nature is supposed not to change, thereby giving a point to the study of history. Yet the context of the thinking (in terms of modern economies and weapon systems) is so very changed that we may have to think in terms of a universe change. In which case history could be more misleading than helpful.

Should people be predictable in order to help others to predict their behavior? Should they signal what they intend to do and then do it? Much the same considerations apply here as they do to secrecy of information.

If we had known it was going to end like this, would we have gone to all that cost and effort? The hindsight answer must very often be 'no'. Because we cannot predict the future we are entitled to place in it any hopes we like, no matter how unrealistic.

The converse of hope is fear. Any designed outcome has to pass the fear test: fear that one party may find itself disadvantaged. It is a poor thing to exchange unlimited hope for a finite fear. That is why it is the local logic of conflict to hold on to promise as long as possible. The designed outcome must also therefore offer promise if it is to attract.

No one can predict the future but we can imagine a range of scenarios. That can be a joint design process. If all the scenarios are unattractive then there is little place to locate that unlimited hope of success. So it can be useful to compare a range of scenarios that have been designed out of available facts and projections. The purpose is to make plain that only a miracle can provide what either side still hopes for. That is one way of narrowing the gap between those different predictions that make us see the same situation very differently.

PERCEPTION

In this section I have covered many of the reasons why people see things differently. They can all be put under the broad heading of 'a difference of perception'. That is why attention to perceptual thinking and an understanding of the nature of perceptual thinking is so very important for conflict thinking. That is why an early section in this book was devoted to the way perception works.

As a final item in this section I ought to add 'perception' in its more pure sense. You look at a cloud and see in it a face; your companion sees the outline of a country. You look at a drawing in a book and see an old woman; a moment later you see a young woman in the same drawing. Exactly the same information input can sometimes be structured in different ways.

In practice it is virtually impossible to separate out this 'pure' type of perceptual difference from the effect of experience, emotion, emphasis and all the other matters listed in this section.

It is enough to note that exactly the same thing, looked at by different people with the same background and motivation, can still be seen in different ways. Once that is accepted then it is easy to accept that at the base of conflict thinking there is often a different way of looking at the same situation: the combatants are in the same physical situation but in a different perceptual situation.

In a later section we shall see how one of the key practical purposes of triangular thinking is to reconcile these different perceptions: by finding common ground or by designing new perceptions that can be adopted by both parties. It is obvious that this needs to be done by a third party since it is almost impossible to change a perception from within that perception.

CHAPTER 6

WHY DO PEOPLE DISAGREE?
BECAUSE THEY WANT DIFFERENT
THINGS

There can be conflict because people see things differently or because they want different things — or a combination of both.

People have different values and objectives. They want to make different choices. Where those choices conflict with the choices of others there is conflict.

As Henry Ford put it so neatly: people could choose any color of car they liked — so long as it was black. That way their freedom of choice would not clash with his economics of manufacturing.

In this section I want to consider the most important way in which people, nations and civilizations make choices. The system is very simple and very practical. It consists of the setting up of rigid guidelines. We know these as values, beliefs, principles and slogans. Once such guidelines are established (gradually or even by fiat) then choice becomes simple. Choices must never go against the guidelines. Choices must be made to fit the guidelines.

An interior decorator is shopping for some wallpaper. She might go through hundreds of samples. She could examine each one to see whether she liked it and whether it would serve her purpose. That would be a lengthy process. The simpler way would be to establish some guidelines from the outset. For example: the paper must have stripes; the paper must have a lot of yellow in it; there must be no red; the price must fall within the budget. These guidelines now help the decorator to go rapidly through the selection procedure. It is now possible immediately to throw out what does not fit the guidelines: for example everything with any red in it. It is also possible for the decorator to ask for, and concentrate her search upon, samples which have the required features. She can ask to be shown only papers with stripes and yellow and in a certain price bracket.

It is obvious that this guideline method is highly convenient. It simplifies decisions.

There is another advantage of the guideline method. The guidelines can be taught and transmitted to others and then used by those others. The decorator could never transfer her entire taste and experience to someone else, but she could easily send an assistant to get samples of striped paper with yellow in it.

It is obvious that this convenient guideline method is the basis of religions, ideologies and civilizations. It has worked very well.

The system is highly convenient but it does make for conflict. When guidelines clash or contradict each other then there is conflict.

STYLE

Contrast a politician with a strong style (de Gaulle or Mrs Thatcher) with a politician without such a readily identifiable style.

The politician with the strong style is readily identifiable. There is a definite image. Each action reinforces that image. Stories (both true and aprocryphal) accumulate around the image. The politician comes to exist much more strongly in the public consciousness. It is true that such politicians may be more easily hated by some, but this itself is an indication of identity. Such politicians are seen to stand for something. In contrast, the politician without style seems weak and grey and bland. Style allows perception to work in a cumulative manner. Without style each incident or action just comes and goes and the person is only as good as the last recorded action. Indeed, a politician without style will be remembered for a visible mistake — because there are few other points of attention. A politician with style can survive many mistakes because there is a different base for the perceptual image. That is why Ronald Reagan came to be known as the 'Teflon President' because mistakes that would have hurt others never seemed to stick to him.

What concerns us here is not so much the image aspect of style but the decision-making aspect. The politician without the strong sense of style will try to make each decision on its own merits. He or she will analyze the matter and discuss it with colleagues. Each decision is a thinking exercise in itself. The politician with style has a very much easier task. He or she just refers the matter to the guideline of the style. The principles behind the style instantly make the decision. It is as simple as the decorator's selection: what action do my guidelines determine at this point? There is no hesitation. Matching something is one of the simplest and swiftest mental operations. There is no need to discuss the matter with others or even to consider it on its merits. Indeed, discussing it with others could only blur the decision since they are not the guardians of the style. There is democracy for the others to make their contribution by acquiescing in the continued exercise of that style. In time they may also find their decisions being made, by them, in accordance with that style. Such decisions will be attributed to the leader and help in the furtherance of the sense of style.

Style permits predictability. A politician with a style is expected to act in accordance with that style. In a sense the style moves ahead of the politician to indicate the decisions and choices that will eventually be made. There is an aspect in which such a style could be said to become a trap, but then any commitment could be looked at in such a manner.

It is obvious that when two leaders with strongly developed styles come into conflict, there will be a stand-off confrontation. Contrary to what many people suppose, this is not due to obstinacy or power politics. Nor is it due to a reluctance to back down or lose. It is more simple. A politician who uses style as a guideline for decision making has *no other way* of making decisions. When a confrontation blocks this type of decision making (because of the clash between styles) neither side has any decision-making capacity. So there is an impasse. But it is an impasse caused by a vacuum, not by stubbornness.

PRINCIPLES

The style of a politician includes the principles which are seen to be guiding the behavior of the politician — even though a great deal is contributed to style by such minor matters as voice, dress and anecdote. The skilled politician packagers in the U.S.A. know their job: they know that brand image can be created and fostered independently of the merit of the product.

By 'principles' I mean those implicit or explicit guidelines for decision. There may be a principle of 'free enterprise' or 'equal opportunity' or 'economic growth'. Some of these will be expressed as slogans. Others will become visible as they are applied. For instance, in any choice between justice and pragmatism, justice will win out (or the other way around).

The principles of the French Revolution (liberty, equality and fraternity) are well known. It is not very likely that they were the motive force behind the revolution. But they did form a convenient crystallization of purpose.

Only rarely does an ideology actually arise from conscious application of the proclaimed principles. These are usually condensed later on as a necessary way of giving identity to the ideology. The fact that they may only be verbalized later does not mean that they have not been operating all the time in an unformulated way. For example, the 'right to be dishonest' and the 'right to be a nuisance' are unformulated principles of Western society. They are more politely expressed as 'freedom'. In the Marxist world the principle that the State takes preference over personal self-interest means well but might be more usefully put as 'the need to be constructive' (in the sense of working towards the good of others as well).

In their collective bargaining exercises, unions need to establish a whole set of principles because these are the only base they have. 'Equal pay for equal work.' 'A fair day's pay for a fair day's work.' 'No cuts in wages under any circumstances.' 'No drop in the standard of living.' Such principles are more than just practical guidelines: they are the very essence of a position. Such principles need not make economic sense. Indeed they can often defeat the very purposes they strive to achieve. For example, a refusal to reduce wages may actually lead to the loss of the job itself (U.S. workers have been much more flexible than European workers in this respect). Yet is is easy to see why principles have to be adhered to.

There is a problem with the sheer continuity of principles. Times may change and principles may need updating or changing. Yet there is no mechanism for doing this. There has to be moment-to-moment continuity. No one dares change a fundamental principle.

For example, the twin principles of job security and equal pay for equal work may have a harmful effect on employment levels. In times of recession, workers have to be laid off and this can be expensive in terms of redundancy money. When times get better corporations are reluctant to take on more workers again and prefer to work below capacity and to turn away orders. We could think of a system to overcome this. New workers would be taken on again at a higher rate than for ordinary workers (say 10% higher wages). But these workers would not immediately have full job security. They would be the first to go if workers had to be laid off — and they would not get the usual redundancy deal. After an agreed time such workers would have to be transferred to the regular work force. Such a concept might well work and might well suit some workers. But it would cut across two basic principles — and so would be unlikely to be tried.

It must be said that the unions' establishment of principles and defense of such principles has been remarkably effective in raising the conditions of employment of workers.

When principles are established by different groups it is obvious that at times there are going to be clashes of principle. But even when principles have been set up by the same group there can still be occasions when two principles meet in contradiction at a particular point. The principle of open-ended health care and the principle of economic husbandry will be in conflict for evermore as the potential and cost of health care grows more rapidly than the means of paying for it. A free enterprise principle of 'non-interference' in business comes to clash with a need to protect investors from insider trading and fraud.

The strange -- and rather absurd — thing about principles is that we set them up as permanent and inviolate and yet know full well that they are going to come into conflict with each other at some time. We just ignore that and hope to deal with it when the time comes. The reason we do this is that the original principles were religious in nature. That meant that they were indeed absolute (like the sanctity of human life). So there was never any point in contemplating a clash of principles. There were also fewer of them. We have tended to treat all subsequent principles in the same unrealistic manner. When conflict arises through a clash of principles we do not know what to do. Here again we need a good deal of design thinking.

When the British force set sail to retake the Falkland Islands some obvious and basic principles were involved. There was the Argentine invasion and the principle that 'aggression cannot be allowed to triumph'. In the course of the negotiations aimed at securing an Argentine withdrawal there was the principle of 'self-determination for the people of the Falklands'. Both these are clear and inviolate principles and Mrs Thatcher acted according to those principles and with the support of the British Parliament.

Let us alter the circumstances a bit. Suppose the islands had been so much nearer the Argentine mainland that Argentine airpower would have been overwhelmingly superior (instead of the islands being at the limit of the range of the planes). Suppose the islands had actually been on the mainland. Suppose the British fleet had already been run down to fit its N.A.T.O. (but not imperial) commitments. Suppose that the U.S.A. had flatly refused any co-operation whatever, in logistics or satellite information.

Now the principles would have remained exactly the same: resisting aggression and self-determination. But the practicality of success of a military expedition would have been greatly altered and even rendered impossible (if it had been a mainland location). So the actual pursuit of a principle has to be tempered by pragmatic considerations.

> 'We shall hold fast to basic principles — and pursue them in such manner as is practicably open to us.'

No one could quarrel with that honest admission because it must be true whether admitted or not. But what is to guide the decision as to 'what is practicable'? That is vital. If we say that no major war is ever practicable any longer, then we need to design new ways of defending principles.

We could phrase the situation a little differently:

> 'We will never abandon these basic principles of resistance to aggression and the right of self-determination.'

Since there is now a principle not to abandon principles, the course of action does not have to follow automatically but can be decided on its own merit (as was probably the case).

SLOGANS

A slogan may encapsulate a principle, a belief or a value. The virtue of a slogan is that it puts into a convenient perceptual package what may otherwise be too vague to provide a reason for doing or thinking.

A good slogan is a substitute for thinking because it provides a multi-purpose conclusion for many different situations.

Most religions have found that fear is the most useful emotion because it is so permanent. You can be frightened of something every minute of your waking life, whereas emotions such as love tend to come and go with all but the most passionate fanatics. Similarly, slogans that are 'against something' are the most durable because their existence is automatically linked to the existence of what they are against. There can, however, be something of a vacuum when the 'enemy' is vanquished and the slogans become meaningless. There may then be a need to create new enemies to maintain the mission of the struggle.

There is no good reason why opposing slogans cannot coexist. It hurts our sense of tidiness and the principle of contradiction — but that is all. It is clear that a decision cannot be made in accordance with two opposing principles — but a slogan is not a decision. Slogans that are 'for' things can as easily coexist as different brand image advertising. We have more difficulty with slogans that are 'against' things because we feel that the 'against' action should be put into effect against other slogans. It does not have to be that way.

VALUES

All human life and all human civilization is about values. With a little reformulation we can show how every conflict is really a clash of values.

Values are very much tied up with principles and with beliefs. There is usually a basic belief from which arises a value. This value is then packaged as a principle.

There are taboo values and direction values. A taboo value is a value that we simply cannot ever negate. For example, the value of life is such a value.

Imagine that a conflict costly in human lives could be avoided if one side accepted the deliberate killing by the other side of a person known by both sides to be innocent. This sacrifice could never be accepted even though thousands more lives (just as innocent) would be lost through this lack of 'pragmatism'. Accepting the proposition would have a lot of local logic but it would breach a taboo value that was regarded as fundamental to civilized society.

63

Direction values are broad compass directions in which we seek to head. We can head 'North' even though from moment to moment our path may need to tack East or West. So there are broad values in 'progress', 'health', 'raise in the standard of living', 'culture and the arts', 'happiness' etc.

Values of both types exist for individuals, for specific groups, for nations and (it is hoped) for humanity. Some of the latter are defined as 'human rights'.

I shall be dealing with values more fully in a later section which treats values as one of the design ingredients in the design of conflict outcomes (values come in both at the input stage and also at the stage of judgment of fit).

At this point I am including values amongst the factors which cause people to want different things. Most people want life but there are circumstances when people seem to want death (suicide, Christian martyrs, Islamic warriors). Value systems can differ enormously.

Curiously we are more ready for a conflict of values than of principles (because, as I have suggested, a principle seems to be an absolute truth). We all know about a person's right to listen to his radio in the open air in the park. That is a value for that person. Then there is the value of silence and peace for other users of the park. So there is a clash of values. The technical solution to this problem (by means of earphones) is a nice example of a designed outcome.

There could be a clash of values between a parent's wish to buy a better education for his children and the state's wish to make educational opportunity equal for all.

As far as possible we handle these value conflicts with two devices. The first is a 'hierarchy of values' which suggests that there are values and values. In the pecking order the higher value will take precedence over the lower one. The second device is that of 'non-interference'. Your enjoyment of a value should not cause disvalue to others. Sydney airport has a curfew so that the convenience of air passengers should not inconvenience the inhabitants in the area who may want to sleep.

We also use 'intention' a great deal. In fact we trade off the value of human life against the practicality of transport. There are about 50,000 road deaths a year in the U.S.A. These could be reduced if everyone drove at the impossibly slow speed of 5 m.p.h. But since the deaths are not 'intended' the trade-off can be made. This whole area gets very tricky. The difference between burning someone with napalm dropped anonymously from a great height and burning them during interrogation torture is one of intention.

It is both frightening and optimistic that values can often be shifted by perception. Looked at in one way something is not attractive. Looked at in another way it becomes attractive. It is frightening because this facility opens the door to any sort of abuse (unless rigid codes like the Geneva Convention prevent it). It is optimistic because it suggests that value clashes can often be sorted out by a design effort which produces an outcome that reconciles the values.

It is interesting how value systems tend to keep separate. The human rights value system is quite separate from the economic value system. There can be no price on the value of a human life. Yet West Germany has been very effective in carrying out money-based deals with East Germany to secure the release of people who want to leave and to ease the traffic flow of visiting relatives across the border. There are obvious dangers of economic blackmail and extortion and also the fundamental disagreeableness of limiting human rights to economic power (like being able to bribe a prison governor to release a prisoner). But before jumping to such obvious conclusions it might be worth exploring the matter more thoroughly. Are we dealing with preferences (which usually have a commercial price) or basic rights (which do not)?

The point I want to emphasize is that we are caught in something of a dilemma. We are conscious that civilization is the sum of its beliefs, values and principles. We are conscious that if we tamper with these for the sake of pragmatism then we may be opening the doors to all sorts of horrors. The horrors arise from acceptance of the principle that 'the end justifies the means' — which itself is used to justify terrorism. Yet we are conscious that the rigid clash of principles and values must be handled in a more imaginative manner than with our current system of naked conflict.

The design idiom is, I believe, our only hope. There is a long way yet to go but our starting on that journey has to be energized by a dissatisfaction with current methods. We cannot look at clashes of principle and value simply as an aberration and a problem that needs to be solved when it arises. We have indeed set up structures like the United Nations which do a good job. For reasons I shall spell out later, I do not feel that this is adequate. There are fundamental flaws in such organizations.

BELIEFS

Perceptions, behavior, values and principles all spring from the underlying beliefs. To discuss the role and importance of beliefs would take a book in itself. I am going to take a rather unusual approach by looking at the physiological basis of beliefs. Why does the mind have to have beliefs? What are beliefs? The suggestion is that beliefs arise inevitably from the particular type of information system we have in our brains. This is the self-organizing system that I described in an earlier section of this book.

Let us look at some different types of 'reality'.

Pragmatic reality: what is the 'cash value' of something, as William James might have said. What effects does this have? What does it bring about? The reality of money is only what it will buy.

Reference reality: something is fixed in terms of reference to other things. A spot is given location on a graph by means of its values along each axis. A ship is fixed at sea by its navigational reference values. We determine a location within a framework.

Equivalence reality: in a mathematical equation, the arrangement on one side is equivalent to the arrangement on the other. This is the reality we use in common language: a concept has a definition. We can move from the concept to the definition or in the other direction.

Testable reality: this is what we sometimes call 'scientific truth'. It is a truth that we can test repeatedly and always get the same answer. What this means is that if we set up the same circumstances again then the same thing will happen.

Circular reality: this is something that follows itself around in a circle. It is circular logic. It is the self-fulfilling prophecy. A transient signal passes but a repeating signal is permanent.

It is the circular type of reality that is involved in beliefs. There is a way of looking at the world which gives a world view which reinforces the way of looking at the world. There is a perceptual lock-in.

As a self-organizing information system, the mind has to make sense of the world around. The loose ends have to be tied up. Where there are gaps then concepts come in to fill the gaps. The whole becomes more and more coherent.

A simple illustration will show how self-organizing systems will always tend to form repeating circular patterns (circular reality).

On a sheet of paper draw about twenty small circles which are separated each from the other. In any way *whatever* draw lines joining up these circles. There may be as many lines as you like going to/from each circle. There must be a minimum of two lines reaching each circle. Now take each circle in turn and place a '1' against any of the lines coming from that circle. Place a '2' against any other line coming from that same circle. Do this for each circle in turn.

The circles represent 'states' and the lines represent a change from one state to another. The figure '1' indicates the preferred path of change. But if this path has been used to reach the circle then path '2' must be used to exit from that circle (second-choice path of change).

Now take a pencil, shut your eyes, and stab the pencil down on the paper. Move the pencil point to the nearest circle. Exit from that circle along the path marked '1' and move along that line to the next circle. Exit from that along path marked '1'. If, however, you have just come in by this path then exit by path marked '2'. Continue in this fashion.

You will find that no matter how you arrange the circles and how randomly you connect them up, nor how randomly you mark the paths, you will *always* end up with a repeating circular path. In other words this apparently random surface has created a 'circular reality' out of a random input.

It is in a similar way that the mind allows experience to organize itself into belief patterns.

This type of internal, circular, perceptual reality is very different from the external, testable, objective reality we are used to in science. But in the world of perception it *is every bit as real*.

Because of the circularity of their nature, beliefs are difficult to remove or alter. Often people will prefer to remain with a belief rather than accept the evidence of their senses. Beliefs do not work in the ordinary logical system. Beliefs can only disappear through atrophy. One point in the circle gets weak and a new path takes over. That is why many of the strongest religions have always insisted on ritual since such ritual actions help to prevent such atrophy.

Although differing belief systems are at the basis of most conflicts, there is no reason why belief systems as such need ever clash. Conflict arises when one belief system believes that its derived values should be applied everywhere and adopts a mission to make this happen. Conflict arises when a belief system has a spread-and-convert mission as part of its belief structure. Conflict arises when one belief system is set up precisely to attack another belief system. None of these 'expansionist' tendencies of belief systems are intrinsic to the nature of beliefs.

CHAPTER 7

WHY DO PEOPLE DISAGREE? BECAUSE THEIR THINKING STYLE ENCOURAGES THEM TO

We have an action-oriented thinking style that favors recognition, discrimination, certainty and permanence. That is the basis of the excellent technical progress that man has made (at different times in different places).

It is not difficult to imagine that a certain thinking style can be very effective for certain purposes and useless for other purposes. It may be worse than useless: it may be dangerous. We know that small scale slash-and-burn agriculture is fine for an underpopulated territory but disastrous for a crowded territory.

This very analogy illustrates one of the problems with our language-based thinking systems. We attach permanent value labels to items and this makes it extremely difficult to regard something as 'good up to a point, but bad beyond that point'. I sometimes call this the 'salt curve'. Some salt on food is good, more salt is very bad.

Our desire for certainty makes us very unhappy with values based on a contingency of circumstance or amount. Most university-style arguments are based on this difficulty. Both parties are usually right, but under different circumstances or in different amounts. Democracy is a 'good thing' and therefore must be introduced wherever possible. If a country is not ready for it or cannot make it work then that is too bad. In any case, to suggest a country is not ready for it is patronizing and paternalistic. Some design effort into transition stages or alternative forms more suited to different cultures might have led to more success.

WORD BASED

Our thinking is word based. In an earlier section I pointed out that word-based thinking has some inevitable disadvantages (such as categorization, permanence and discrimination). Language was never designed as a thinking medium. The purpose of language is communication. It is quite wrong to suppose that the requirements of communication and the requirements of thinking are the same. Why should they be the same?

With a communicating medium we strive to remove all doubt and the purpose of each further word is to help in that direction. With thinking we want to open up possibilities and connections in order to allow insights to form. Poetry is much more of a thinking idiom than is prose. Prose describes what is. Poetry indicates what can be.

Words come to be laden with emotional values and once so laden can never be cleansed. Words are a living accumulation of our history and through them we become trapped in idioms which are long past their usefulness. The word 'profit' cannot, in many societies, ever be rehabilitated to signify the surplus required for investment in production. The word 'manipulate' can never be rehabilitated to mean the beneficial placement of an individual so that he or she is able to do the best (for themselves).

There are many new concepts that we need to develop but cannot because there is no suitable way of launching the appropriate word. Any new word will be treated as a gimmick by those who do not understand how poor language really is in describing system behavior. In an earlier section I mentioned the need for a new word that would describe something that made good local logical sense but bad larger logical sense.

I invented the term 'lateral thinking' many years ago because there was a desperate need to describe the logic of creativity and the logic of pattern changing in a self-organizing information system. This activity of changing perceptions and concepts is not happily lumped with artistic production under the broad term 'creativity'.

In this book I am attempting to introduce the expression 'triangular thinking' to describe the needed third-party role in conflict thinking and the definition of that role.

POLARIZATION

Since we need to make action decisions we do not like people who sit on the fence. We do not like economists who carry one view in one hand and the opposite view in the other hand. The founder of Christianity was quite fierce about 'lukewarm' people.

Thinking is a dynamic process. You can move dynamically in a direction but not in opposite directions at the same time.

There is a way around this apparent dilemma of polarization. It is the 'compartment' method used by the Japanese in their ordinary life. During

69

the day there is a Western-style business executive. In the evening (when in Japan) there is a Japanese-style executive. At home there is a traditional Japanese family man.

Instead of being somewhere between a socialist and a capitalist every day of the week — and being called a Liberal — you could be a capitalist on Mondays, Wednesdays and Saturdays and a socialist on the remaining days. In a way this is what the Swedish economy has had the good sense to do.

No doubt there are many politicians who feel that in some of their decisions they are socialist and in some they are capitalist (this is not quite as good as the compartment method which enjoys full consistency in each compartment). But language is not happy with this and, because language is not happy with it, political support for it is weak.

Language could never have been designed to tell us that the red berry is poisonous on Monday and Friday but excellent on other days.

TRUTH AND FALSITY

I have touched on these matters in the section on argument and dialectic thinking.

Bad logic makes for bad thinking. There is no problem with that.

Good logic makes for good thinking. There is a big problem with that. Good logic, like a functioning computer, is only a servicing device to make sense of the perceptions presented to it. Excellence of logic can never make up for inadequacy of perception. But excellent logic does give quite a false sense of certainty and arrogance and righteousness. We really do believe that a line of argument without logical error must be right. It can never be any more than consistent with our starting positions which are themselves determined by perception.

There is also the notion of one truth, like one winner in a race. If you feel you have the winner then what are other people claiming to offer?

I have mentioned elsewhere the limiting notion that you need to be right at every step in your thinking. This is only true if you are going to justify your end position solely by the route of derivation (how you got there). If, however, the end position is going to have to justify itself then the route there does not matter. This is always the case with design. You can never justify a design by your thinking steps. The justification always has to take the form of a final assessment: does the design carry out the intended purpose and does it fit the acceptance profile?

I recognize the value of truth and falsity as fully as anyone else, but I also recognize that an obsession with step-by-step truth can only work in closed systems.

Consider a whole range of other responses that can be used in a discussion.

'That is interesting.'
'That leads on to . . .'
'This is tentative.'
'At this point this is speculative.'
'Here is a provocation.'
'There is no justification yet for looking at it this way but . . .'

Once we understand the nature of patterning systems then there is an *absolute logical need* for these sorts of remarks. In the asymmetry of a patterning system we may need to move to another part of the pattern because only from there can we see, in hindsight, what will immediately become logical. The old-fashioned insistence on truth at each step is simply false.

THE PRINCIPLE OF CONTRADICTION

The principle of contradiction is the basis of our usual logical system. Two mutually exclusive statements cannot both be true. Something cannot be both true and false at the same time.

In a sense this principle of contradiction is carried straight over into our conflict thinking. Two mutually exclusive desires cannot both be accommodated at the same time. You cannot go North and South at the same moment. So there has to be a conflict to see which desire triumphs.

A conflict is sometimes treated like a race. There is one race and one first prize. We cannot have a situation in which both John and Peter win the race. The two statements: 'John won the race' and 'Peter won the race' are contradictory.

Our style of thinking is such that we deliberately *search out* such contradictions because that is the usual way we make progress in our thinking. So instead of avoiding such contradictions or reducing them to the minimum we try to put everything in contradictory terms.

'All swans have long necks.'
'This bird does not have a long neck.'
'Therefore this bird cannot be a swan.'

The two statements: 'this bird is a swan' and 'this bird has a short neck' would be contradictory and therefore the bird cannot be a swan. This is normal thinking behavior.

In order to support this type of thinking we have to use complete and exclusive categories. We have to say: 'all swans have long necks' — which we can do easily because we can choose to use the term swan only for birds with long necks. The system would not work at all if we were to use terms like 'largely' or 'usually' or 'by and large'.

'By and large swans have long necks.'
'This bird does not have a long neck so it is unlikely to be a swan but I cannot be sure.'

That seems much less satisfactory.

Yet in conflict thinking it might be very helpful to switch from rigid terms to such terms as 'usually', 'on the whole' and 'by and large'. These convey the same meaning without being vulnerable to attack. Immediately the principle of contradiction must be replaced by one of 'likelihood'. There is absolutely no harm in this. There was only harm when dialectic was used to defend a constructed theology. To say: 'God may be perfect' is not the same as saying 'God is perfect' because you could not then proceed to all the needed deductions.

'This cloth is green.'
'No, it is blue.'
'Bring it into the light.'
'It is still blue.'

Quite possibly the cloth was iridiscent: both green and blue at the same time. There is no reason, except contradiction, why the people of Northern Ireland should not be both British and Irish at the same time. Berlin is a working example of an apparent contradiction: a city in the middle of a different country — and a hostile one at that. Yet it works quite well.

We are much too frightened of apparent contradictions. We back off as soon as we spot a contradiction because this is how we have been trained to do our thinking. It would be a great help in the design mode of conflict thinking if we were to accept apparent contradictions and then to move forward from them. Are they really contradictions? Is there any way we can modify the situation to allow the contradiction to exist in a practical sense? In the end we might have to let the contradiction go — but only right at the end.

If necessary we can always protect the contradiction with the new word 'po' that I invented and which I shall describe in a later section. 'Po' is used with provocations to indicate that a statement is offered *outside* the judgment system. We might say 'Po, wheels should be square' and then proceed to develop some very interesting ideas.

Consistency is tied up with contradiction. People are not supposed to contradict themselves. One statement they make is supposed to be consistent with another. Yet people should be able to change their minds and their positions. There may be new information or a change of circumstance, or two inconsistent statements may be held simultaneously. Public opinion polls very often show this. There is a majority in favor of U.S. involvement in Central America. Yet there is, at the same time, a majority against every suggested form of involvement.

A wife may want her husband to earn more money and at the same time not want him to go abroad on money-making trips. Both wants are genuine even if logically contradictory. We need to look at the substance of what is suggested, not the form. It is over-attention to the logical consistency of form that so often makes conflicts insoluble.

It may be felt that if we were to devalue the principle of contradiction there would be total chaos. In this chaos anything would go and it would be impossible to reach any conclusions at all. It might just end up as a parallel mouthing of slogans and desires. This does not follow at all. There may indeed be times when conflict thinking is nothing more than a shouting of slogans and accusations, but that happens now if the parties want it to be that way.

A carpenter who makes a table goes steadily about his craft, putting the pieces together until he has the completed whole. That carpenter is not using the principle of contradiction. He finds that pieces can be fitted together and that a joint can be made in a certain way. This is a positive principle: it fits, it works out, it can be done. This is the principle of construction. It is a perfectly usable principle.

We should note very carefully that our obsession with the principle of contradiction derives from theological argument in which it was necessary *to prove a heresy to be false*. The principle of contradiction is essential for this purpose. This is not the case with all other types of conflict thinking. In this book the emphasis is on the design idiom. That is obviously a constructive idiom — similar to that of the carpenter and the table.

We need to be very clear about this point. If we are obsessed by the principle of contradiction then we are condemned to the negative exclusion type of thinking. We need to escape from this obsession in order to develop the positive constructive type of thinking: the design idiom.

CHAPTER 8

WHY DO PEOPLE DISAGREE?
BECAUSE THEY ARE SUPPOSED TO

Conflict is an expected and revered idiom in our civilization. I do not just mean the expected heroics of defending the motherland against aggressors, or coming to the aid of the victims of a bully. It may have been necessary that the appropriate honor and glory were attached to such activities — and that may still be necessary. Extraordinary sacrifices have been made (on whichever side) and they should be rightly honored. The spectrum spans from such attitudes towards conflict right across to the competitive rivalry between two tennis players.

There are times when conflict may be necessary. There are times when it may be enjoyable as competition. I do not intend to argue the merits of each case. Nor have I set out in this book to condemn conflict as such. I am concerned with *the thinking about conflict*. I am concerned with those areas where we want to resolve conflict and are not at all happy with our means for doing so.

The point I want to make in this section is that our civilization is highly geared up for conflict. The idioms pervade our attitudes, our expectations and our language. There are huge gaps in our culture when it comes to conflict resolution. We like to talk about peace but can only think of *fighting our way there*.

LANGUAGE INADEQUACY

At many points in this book I come back to this same point. The more I get involved in thinking about thinking the more conscious I become of the inadequacy of even a rich language like English. Either words simply do not exist, or they wreck an intended meaning by coupling it with a misleading one, or they are emotionally loaded.

It is perfectly true that there is sufficient flexibility in language to express new thoughts by putting together old words in carefully crafted ways. That

74

is, after all, what I am trying to do in this book and have tried to do in previous books. But it is not good enough.

It is possible to describe a new concept with a collection of words. This adequately serves a descriptive, explanatory or communication function.

'Go into the warehouse and bring me out the structure which has a flat top and is supported by four legs, one at each corner.'

You know what I mean and you would bring me a table. My description and communication is perfect. But that description does not create the *concept* of a table. We may use the adequate description as often as we like and a concept may or may not eventually form. We can understand why this is so by considering both the mathematics of combination and the nature of the self-organizing system of perception — as I described it in an earlier section. Obviously concepts could not form for every temporary collection of words.

But until a concept has formed then that idea cannot really enter into our thinking. A concept is like a road junction. Around that junction a small town develops. The town grows. It gets suburbs. New roads form to other towns. The town gets an identity. You can go from there to other places. That is what a concept is like. But a description is only like a temporary travel itinerary. You can use it accurately but that is all.

So it is simply not good enough for language purists to say that we do not need new words because our present words are adequate enough to *describe* anything. Description is not good enough.

We have a multitude of words for victory, defeat, surrender, gain, loss, attack, defend, win, lose etc. There is no shortage of concepts here.

Let us now look at the concepts available to describe conflict resolution. We can have back down, defeat, surrender, give up — and their reciprocals on the winning side. We can have compromise, truce or moratorium. These are all unsatisfactory because they do not indicate that there is a satisfactory outcome: there is just a cessation of hostilities. The word 'peace' does not come in here because it is not a description of the outcome but of a state that may be reached after the outcome has been decided. Peace may follow victory or it may follow defeat.

I would like a concept to indicate the following:

'We had this conflict and we did some constructive thinking about it. As a result we have designed an outcome with which both sides are very happy. It is not just a toleration or acceptance of that outcome but we actually see positive benefits for both parties in the designed outcome.'

How do we express such a concept? How do we describe any conflict resolution that is highly satisfactory? It is clear that language has never been much concerned with such matters because culture expects win/lose conflicts.

Let us take another example. We have many words for friends and enemies. We have many words for a variety of relationships between friends and enemies: love, hate, antagonism, trust, suspicion etc. Let us look, however, at a gap. I want a word to describe the following concept:

> 'This fellow is my enemy. I know he wants to destroy me just as much as I want to destroy him. But I can communicate with him and work with him. Together we can work constructively on matters which can only benefit from such co-operation.'

In other words, an enemy I like and can work with constructively. I do not even have to 'like' him; respect would be enough. Even without respect I can still want to communicate and co-operate constructively. This idea of 'an enemy I want to work with' is quite contrary to normal language because it violates the principle of contradiction which I mentioned in a previous section.

In this book I shall be introducing the concept of 'triangular thinking'. There is need for such a word to discuss the following concept:

> 'In a conflict situation the two parties are unable to stand outside their own perceptions. In order to move from the argument mode to the design mode there is need for a third party. This third party is not a go-between, negotiator or mediator. The third party acts as a mirror, an overview, a provider of provocation and creativity and a director of thinking. The third party also organizes the mapping of the situation. This third party is an integral part of the design thinking required for conflict resolution.'

That is a lot to have to say each time. It would be much more convenient to talk of 'triangular thinking' for the whole process. Unfortunately it is not enough just to say 'third party'. A third party could be a judge who is in a superior position. A third party could also be a low-level negotiator who fetches and carries between the parties. What I need to imply is a third party who is on the same level as the other parties and is there to carry out — with them — the design thinking. The triangle gives an instant impression of an equality of angles. A triangle also gives the impression (if it is drawn in the normal upright way) of the third party standing above the conflict — so implying neutrality and an overview of the thinking that is taking place.

It is astonishing that we do not have the word 'confliction' for the setting up, encouraging and promotion of conflict. We may believe that conflicts just happen to arise. We do need a word for those occasions when there is an active effort to create a conflict. More importantly we need the word 'de-confliction' which deals with the dissipation, or resolution, of a conflict. De-confliction is more than just resolution for it is the designing away of the basis for the conflict.

ENCOURAGEMENT

It is the spectators who urge on the gladiators. It is the football crowds that energize the players.

When the war fleet set sail for the Falklands there was an extraordinary gung-ho spirit, almost like the send-off of a Crusade. There was a clear aggressor who had done wrong. A well-trained professional army was being sent to teach a lesson to a presumptuous upstart country. It was all going to take place far away so there would be no bombing and no rationing. There was a certainty of victory. Under such circumstances, the natural enjoyment of conflict (when victory is certain) came to the fore. Conflict is enjoyable.

In August 1984 the miners' strike in England was still going on. Parliament in Westminster had just had its final session before the summer break. On August 1 *The Daily Telegraph* newspaper had the following headline:

'Labour savaged on pit strike
MPS HAIL THATCHER TRIUMPH'

On the back page there was another headline:

'BENN BEATEN TO QUIVERING PUREE'

(referring to a Labour Party spokesman with a reputation for sharp attack and far-Left views).

This is good knockabout stuff. It is the rough and tumble of parliament. It is the essence of party politics. It is the basis of democracy.

Just consider how dull it would have been if there had been but a small paragraph, somewhere in the paper, to note that a group of senior people —from both parties — had met to design a constructive and practical outcome to the crisis which had been going on for many weeks and was costing about £10 million a day.

It has to be said that newspapers have a job to do. The encouragement of conflict is of much greater interest than its resolution, just as a sex murder is of much more interest than the uneventful life of a secretary.

At the time of the Vietnam War the American press discovered the joys of crusading: having a mission and having people on your side. Those joys were compounded by the Watergate crisis in the Nixon administration. Then came Carter and the Iranian hostage problem (amongst others). At this point the press had become unstoppable. It is to the credit of President Reagan that he redressed the whole situation by ignoring the press and going directly to the people via television. His charm, sincerity, appearance and acting experience no doubt helped a great deal. Once the television audiences could see and judge for themselves (even if they judged incorrectly) there was no point in the press calling him an incompetent monster. The joys of crusading were over.

The point about this diversion is that it is the nature of the press (and not an abuse of it) to foster and encourage conflict with the appropriate noises and divisiveness. That is not, however, the nature of television, where the protagonists can speak for themselves and where stridency seems absurd. Indeed, television may be the most anti-conflict medium yet. The conflict-exciting demagogic speeches of a crowded hall are ridiculous with the living-room intimacy of television.

On the whole, however, it is in the nature of society to encourage and spur on conflict right up to the point at which it becomes personally inconvenient. By then it can be too late to switch it off.

There is an enjoyment of conflict because there is an enjoyment both of fighting and of competition. Even when the motives are of the purest there is still an enjoyment of the mission, purpose and camaraderie of protest marches.

Life is dull and conflict adds drama and excitement. Conflict makes us interested in finding out what happens next (which is why people remained glued to their radios throughout the action in the Falkland Islands). Conflict is interesting to talk about — everyone can take sides and be an expert.

For a whole variety of reasons we do encourage conflict both explicitly and implicitly. It is difficult to encourage one type of conflict and to discourage another because the language, idioms and attitudes spill across from the beneficial sort to fuel the destructive sort.

Children like bang-bang cartoons not because they are bloodthirsty but because a dead person is the simplest form of achievable dramatic action. Something has happened. Just as money is no more than a score-keeping system for a rich man, so a tally of dead bodies is the simplest way to keep score for any hero.

PART III CREATIVITY, DESIGN AND THE THIRD PARTY ROLE

CHAPTER 9

DESIGN

In this section I am going to discuss the design idiom. The section is certainly not a complete treatise on this very important subject. I do, however, want to contrast the design idiom with the argument idiom that I have discussed in a previous section.

'How do we exclude this?' Here we have the negative exclusion of the argument idiom.

'How do we achieve this?' Here we have the positive construction of the design idiom.

It needs saying that designing a conflict outcome is significantly more difficult than designing a piece of machinery. This is because human nature is unpredictable. We do know enough about physical laws to be able to predict that something should work (we can even calculate it mathematically). But we do not know enough about human behavior to predict whether something will work.

Many years ago I trained a group of youngsters from a local high school in the south of Sweden. This group was then presented with problems by various people from the Government and from industry. The experiment was organized by Gunnar Wessman, a leading Swedish industrialist and a great believer in lateral thinking. One of the presented problems concerned the weekend shift in a chemical plant. No one wanted to work the weekend shift. How could workers be motivated to work the weekend shift?

The youngsters came up with a direct and innocent approach. Forget about motivating the workers. Employ a special weekend work force which would permanently work over the weekends. When this was suggested no one welcomed it as a good idea. It was felt the unions would not permit it and, in any case, who would want such a job? In the event it turned out to be a success. Moreover there were many times as many applicants for the job as were required.

So there is the special difficulty that an idea which would have worked may not be accepted.

UN-DESIGN

We can take it that many conflicts are designed by history, by circumstance, by mood and by moment-to-moment developments. We can also take it that many conflicts are designed (not necessarily deliberately) by the parties involved, who focus on differences and crystallize conflict points.

The process of *un-design* involves unraveling the strands that have come together in this way and seeking to put them together in another way.

EXAGGERATION

Two parties see the same situation in a slightly different way. This is, of course, the major basis of conflict. Different perceptions lead to different desires and action choices. Each party chooses its own route. There is now a conflict about the choice of route. Although the actual difference of route may be slight it can end up as a full-blown conflict with apparently diametrically opposed views.

A husband and wife argue as to the best route to take to drive to a friend's house. Each of them selects a different route. There is a fierce argument because it is now a complete battle of wills: a choice of route A or route B. All sorts of other things get drawn into the argument. When we start to un-design the argument we find that the actual difference of routes is very small indeed.

It is a tragedy of the argument mode that once there is a complete disagreement it does not matter how trivial the point may be. The conflict is immediately a complete one — with totally opposing wishes.

BACK TO BACK

It is amazing how dialects can differ sharply between two villages which are only half a mile apart. It seems impossible that this language difference could have emerged, or could survive, when communication between the two villages seems so easy. There is, however, a very good explanation which has a lot of relevance to the un-design of conflicts.

Imagine two major centers which are many miles apart and therefore develop their own dialects. There is very little communication between these centers. From these centers there is a spread of population. Peripheral villages develop around each center. These spread farther and farther out. Since the people in these villages have originally come from the major centers they always tend to travel to the major center from which their family started. Communication is always centripetal towards the center of origin. As the rings of villages spread further there comes a time when the two rings get very close to each other. So a village that is on the outermost ring of the first center may actually be only half a mile from a village on the outermost ring of the second center. The villages are very close to each other and yet each keeps the very different dialect of its own original center. This is the 'back-to-back' phenomenon.

The same thing happens with conflict. Two ideologies may start very far apart. With time each develops and changes. Eventually the sharply polarized differences no longer actually exist. The positions are in reality very close, as with the back-to-back villages. Yet this closeness of position cannot be seen because all ideological communication is thought of through the original centers. This is the case with various shades of Christianity. In due course it will probably happen with capitalism and socialism. Each gets closer and closer to the other. There is more central direction of capitalism and more welfare concern. There is a greater emphasis on initiative and enterprise in socialism.

It is always possible to show great divides by focusing on the historic points of difference which are forever frozen as principles: capitalism puts the emphasis on the individual, socialism on the state. It is always useful to keep such principles in mind. Yet on particular occasions the interests of both parties may be very closely aligned and it is a bad mistake to separate those interests by working through the original points of difference.

So the very common 'back-to-back' phenomenon must be kept in mind when un-designing conflicts.

OBJECTIVES AND BENEFITS

In a later section I shall deal in more depth with objectives, benefits and values. For the moment I want to focus on how a particular objective is chosen because it seems to offer a certain benefit. The objective itself then becomes the focus of the conflict and the benefit is forgotten.

In the prolonged metalworkers' strike in Germany in 1984, the unions were demanding a reduction in working hours from 40 a week to 35. The management resisted this because it was felt that production would suffer. So the conflict centered on the conflicting objectives: 35-hour week against a 40-hour week. But the sought-for benefits were quite different. Management did not want the 'disbenefit' of a fall in production. Unions wanted the benefit of more leisure time (and the possibility of increasing employment by reducing working hours). Management might have suggested a scheme of 1 week on 40 hours and the next on 35 hours and a comparison of output production. From this comparison a choice of working hours could have been made. Management might have invited the unions to help show how a reduction in hours could be used to increase employment. For their part the unions could have asked that any increase in productivity should be reflected first in shorter working hours rather than in more profits. It was only the very simple crystallization of the conflict around the 35/40-hour working week that created the problem. Once the conflict had been posed this way then the very unimaginative solution (38½-hour week) was inevitable. This solves the conflict for the moment but merely sets the stage for the next round of conflict.

So it is important to distinguish the real values and benefits from the declared objectives. Otherwise a conflict may crystallize around these declared objectives which are, after all, only one way of delivering the values.

CONTRADICTORY DESIRES

There are some conflicts which are designed by the parties involved to be insoluble. The conflict in Northern Ireland is of this type. If one party in a conflict will only be happy if the other party is made unhappy — and vice versa — then there is a problem of contradiction. It may only be soluble by making both parties unhappy, which is much easier than making both parties happy.

It is necessary to isolate and define these contradictory points in order to try to get rid of them. By definition, any desire put forward by one party cannot contain a desire to do down the other party. There has to be a clear statement of wishes that must stand on their own. Desires must be stated as positives.

I am not suggesting that this process is easy or that it will always work. Where it does not work then other approaches must be tried. These might include transitional steps, introduction of new elements, change in setting, creation of significant advantages for both sides and so on.

Where, however, it is possible to get the conflicting aims redefined in a positive way, this can change an impossible conflict into a soluble one.

PERCEPTUAL CLASH

As I have repeated several times, a difference of perception is at the bottom of many conflicts. A school expels a boy for truancy. The parents see this as no more than enterprise on the part of the youngster. The school sees it as deliberate disobedience and a threat to school discipline.

The Falklands invasion is seen by Britain as naked aggression which has to be resisted. By the Argentinians the occupation of the Malvinas is seen only as an acceleration of an inevitable process when negotiations seemed never to get anywhere. The two views are clearly incompatible and yet both are right in their way.

One design approach would be to seek to accommodate both views. The Argentine aggression would have been reversed by the withdrawal of troops and perhaps some compensation to the Islanders. At the same time there would be a guaranteed commitment by Great Britain to negotiate the future of the Islands within a certain time limit. In practice this approach could have been carried through in the following manner. The U.S.A. could have come out firmly on the side of Britain and offered full military support. The overwhelming military might would have made it obvious to Argentina that resistance was pointless. In return the U.S.A. would have insisted that Great Britain seriously negotiate the future of the Islands within a time limit. As it was the Argentinians had some hope of humiliating Britain militarily (or thought they might have) and this was attractive. Also, if they withdrew unconditionally then the whole adventure was a total defeat.

Obviously the wishes of the Islanders would have to be paramount. But wishes do not exist in a vacuum. They take place in a setting. It must be clear to the Islanders that the day will come when Britain is simply not able to defend them militarily no matter how much she might like to. Nor can they rely on Mrs Thatcher, and her style of decision, being in power forever.

COMMON ELEMENTS

Another approach to perceptual clash is to see if a design can be based on the common elements in the two perceptions. There is a focusing on the areas of agreement rather than disagreement (the A.D.I. mapping tool was mentioned earlier: areas of agreement, disagreement and irrelevance).

In the example of the truant schoolboy, the common elements might be: that truancy is not compatible with school discipline; that enterprise is a useful personality characteristic. The designed outcome could therefore be some punishment other than expulsion and the provision of a more suitable enterprise outlet. Alternatively the school principal might have recommended the boy be transferred to another school which offered more enterprise opportunities instead of expelling the boy.

PERCEPTION SHIFT

Where this works, this is the most effective mechanism of all. There is an attempt to bring about an actual shift in perception so that something is seen in a different way. The shift is a creative or insight shift: what is sought by lateral thinking.

In an ordinary strike situation both sides show their determination and strength through a sort of auction of flagellation: if we suffer so much we must be determined. The system is a good one and it does work. Suppose the system was redesigned so that determination and suffering could still be used but that at the end there was not a total loss of production. Workers would continue working for a reduction in pay. The factory would make no profits at all. The profits and part of the workers' pay would be diverted to a special escrow fund. This accumulating fund would now form part of the ultimate bargaining position and could be divided according to the settlement. In this way production would continue and markets would not be lost. Nevertheless both sides would be hurt. If it was felt that the hurt was not enough then the amount of pay reduction and the fraction of factory income diverted into the escrow account could be increased. This design would provide the apparent contradiction of a strike and yet full production at the same time (I shall deal with this aspect of contradiction later).

The important point here is a perception shift that sees loss of production as not being in the workers' long-term interests.

It is unrealistic to suppose that one party will suddenly see things the same way as the other party and declare the conflict to be over. The perception change may indeed occur but it cannot be made manifest as such. The designed outcome can be based on such a perception change but must offer something new.

For example, the perception shift towards recognizing automation as being in the workers' interest rather than against it needs to be accompanied by a structure in which workers actually get to own (through leasing) the automation equipment.

SUB-ELEMENTS

A basic design idiom is to break down the apparent ingredients into sub-elements. A child playing with a set of Lego construction blocks will dismantle all preformed pieces in order to build up again from the most basic elements. So in a conflict situation we survey the ingredients: values, objectives, positions, channels, mechanisms, personalities etc. An attempt is then made to construct the needed design.

For example, in the downing of the Korean airliner there are all sorts of sub-elements involved: defense, warning, mistake, guilt, callousness, public opinion etc. One approach might have been for the Russians to reiterate that they had a very tight air defense system and that the same thing might well happen again. Nevertheless they accepted some responsibility for the event and were therefore prepared to pay some compensation to the families of those killed — provided the Koreans matched this compensation because they had also contributed to this 'military accident'. Here we have the concept of an accident that is regrettable and should be avoided but is a coming together of different elements (like a car hitting an oil patch on a road).

From the Russian point of view no mistake was committed by them. The mistake was on the part of the erring pilot. After all, if a coach driver misses a curve and takes his passengers into a ravine then it is the coach driver's fault. The other point of view is that if a planeload of innocent passengers was knowingly shot down there cannot be any justification for that.

Any concept, desire or position is always made up of sub-elements. What is involved here? What are the elements? Why do we want to do this? Once the sub-elements have been teased out then an assembly type of design can take place.

CENTRAL CONFLICT POINT

It would seem natural to resolve a conflict by resolving the central point in the belief that this is the true basis of the conflict. This is a wrong approach for a number of reasons.

The central conflict point is often only a convenient perceptual crystallization of the conflict and is not the basic cause at all. So a designed outcome that treats this point may yet be unacceptable to both sides.

The central conflict point will be the most fiercely defended because it is seen as the core point. To surrender this core point is to accept defeat. So to attack the central point is like setting out to capture the enemy's standard from the very first.

The alternative approach is to leave the central conflict point alone and to work around on everything else. It often happens that at the end the central point becomes so unsupported that it can be abandoned quietly without fuss. This approach might seem to be 'avoiding the issue' but in fact it is an attempt to change the setting in which the issue has any relevance.

WORKING BACKWARDS

This is one of the most powerful ways of working out a design. We start out with the end point and then see what alternative circumstances might get us there. Then for each of these we see what circumstances could get us to that point. We follow this procedure all the way back. In the end we have a wide fan of starting points. Each of these starting points could provide a route to the designed end.

For example, if our intention was to 'cope with a water shortage', the points that could lead us there might include: more supplies; substitution; saving; doing without. If we then take the point 'saving', we find that we could get there by: restricting supplies; rationing; changed habits; reducing apparatus waste, etc. If we looked at 'changed habits' this could be achieved by: education; public information; monitoring. In a water shortage in New York, a saving of 90 million gallons a day was effected. This was largely due to publicity efforts by Mayor Koch, who appeared frequently on television and made all children in the city into 'deputy mayors' with responsibility for controlling water waste in their homes.

In childhood books there is often the puzzle of three boys fishing. From each rod there is a line. The lines get involved in a considerable tangle. One line ends up attached to a fish. Which boy has got the fish? You can follow the lines down from each boy in turn until you reach the fish. Smart children soon figure out that if you start with the fish then you can trace the line back to the lucky boy with ease. Working backwards is roughly the same principle. It is a powerful method. But it does have one great drawback. What is the end point? In a creative design we do not *yet know* what the end point is likely to be. If we think we know what the end point is then we are just working towards a very routine solution.

DREAM SOLUTION

This is another basic approach to design. It can provide the end point for the 'working backwards' method and it can also be used in its own right as a design idiom.

We simply jump to the end and conceive a 'dream solution'. Because it is a dream solution it can contain illogicalities. More importantly it can put forward circumstances under which the conflict would no longer exist. For example, if we accepted a concept of 'marginal work' then the 1984 miners' strike would not have taken place. This concept might hold that up to 10% of work in a changing industry might be marginal at any time. So the 'uneconomic pits' might stay open provided that their fraction of the whole (measured in costs, production or any other way) did not exceed 10%. This would give a sort of buffer and predictability. If more pits became uneconomic then some would indeed close down.

It may not be much use saying 'if the price of coal were to rise considerably then there would be no problem' because that is like saying 'if there were no problem then there would be no problem'. It would be permissible to say: 'if we knew the price of coal were going to rise in the future then . . .' as a change in circumstance. That might lead to notions of investing in coal futures or using coal as an investment commodity.

CHANGE IN CIRCUMSTANCE

This is another powerful way of designing a conflict outcome. If the circumstances change then the whole locked-in psychology might also change. At the time of the Iranian hostage crisis I was asked on television in New York what I would suggest. It was not a matter for which I had a ready-made answer. So I had to give an off-the-cuff answer. I said that it seemed to me that the main point in the Iranian students holding the hostages was that this considerably upset the U.S.A. If 'somehow' the U.S.A. could signal patience and that it would not be blackmailed in this manner, then there would be little point in holding the hostages. Such a signal would seem very callous and uncaring for the hostages (although it might have secured their earlier release). So I suggested that each hostage would receive $1,000 a day from the U.S. Government as compensation for this unfair imprisonment. Each day a hostage would know that something beneficial had happened and that patience had some reward at least. This suggestion was picked up in the New York Village Voice and also debated in the U.S. Senate. It was felt that it would be too expensive a precedent in terms of future prisoners of war. This, of course, completely missed the special psychological basis of the suggestion — which was to signal patience. At that time the total compensation would have amounted to half the cost of a helicopter.

IF CLAUSES

These are related to both dream solutions and also to circumstance changes. We set out to make one small speculative change: 'if such and such were the case . . .'. This can serve both to clarify the basis of the conflict and also to help design a solution.

I should point out that I am *not* referring here to future possibilities and scenarios (if these should happen) but to alterations in the conditions of the conflict.

'If the miners could be defined as a permanent special case . . .'

Then there would be no need to use them as a test case to impose industrial discipline.

The point about a conflict is that the perceptions and thinking have locked themselves solid. Therefore there is a need to introduce some instability in order to unfreeze the thinking.

BLOCKS, TABOOS AND ASSUMPTIONS

It is a common negotiating tactic to state right at the beginning that certain things are 'not negotiable' and then to seem very willing to discuss other matters. It needs to be made quite clear that when the design mode is used this approach is not acceptable.

'Nothing is going to be excluded from the design considerations. When we come to the designed output you can reintroduce these matters if you so wish.'

To accept boundaries and limitations from the beginning makes design impossible. A design brief can contain limitations but these are then considered later. It is a fundamental design point to always work back into boundaries rather than only to work *within* boundaries from the beginning.

UP OR DOWN DESIGN

Sculptors work in one of two ways.

A sculptor may take a block of marble and then work downwards from a broad outline until in the end the detail is introduced. So a designer may start with a broad notion of the designed outcome and may then work downwards from this to the final detail.

A sculptor may also take a wire armature and then proceed to build up his figure by adding small bits of clay at a time. This is the building-up approach. Each added piece has to be justified. It is more an assembly type.

In both cases the sculptor has some overall vision. The assembly approach may, however, allow the sculptor at each moment to consider what has been added and to remove it if it does not fit.

In terms of the design of conflict outcomes the assembly approach may seek to solve pieces at a time and then to put the whole together. The 'down' approach starts with a broad picture and then works downwards to meet values and objectives.

THE CORE APPROACH

This is another design idiom. Here the designer fashions some central 'core' principle and then builds the design around this. Note that this core principle is quite separate and distinct from the central conflict point. The core principle is not an attempt to neutralize this central conflict point.

For example, in looking at the future of the Falkland Islands the core principle might be:

> 'The Islanders must have an attractive option which does not hold Great Britain hostage.'

SUMMARY

In this section I have done no more than touch on some design idioms and aspects. In practice design is a mixture of provocation, dreams and perceptual shifts together with methodical working out of means and methods.

I want to emphasize that the design approach is based on a thorough exploration and mapping of the situation as described in a previous section under the term 'Think-2'. Such a mapping is essential.

As I mentioned previously, a design always has two purposes. It must do what it is supposed to do and it must be acceptable to the clients.

In the case of designed outcomes to conflict situations the two purposes become very close because the design ingredients are themselves the values, desires, priorities and fears of the conflicting parties. So it is not a matter of creating an abstract design and then presenting this to the parties. That is why I have emphasized in this book the concept of 'triangular thinking'. This indicates that all three parties (the opposing parties and the third party) are involved as a design team.

It is essential, however, that the conflicting parties realize that when they are taking part in the designed outcome exercise the argument mode is excluded. In order to insure this the third party takes something of a 'conducting' role in the exercise. This corresponds to the superior angle of the triangle. For the design mode to be of value it must be used properly.

CHAPTER 10

WHY DISPUTANTS ARE IN THE WORST POSITION TO SOLVE THEIR DISPUTE

It is natural to assume that the parties involved in a conflict should settle their conflict. It is their business. Their interests are at stake. They started it anyway.

Unfortunately, the parties involved in a dispute happen to be in the worst possible position to settle that dispute. That creates an awkward dilemma. It is as if the only person in the position to rescue a drowning person is someone who cannot swim. Or as if the only people motivated to be engineers are those incapable of doing mathematics.

There is one — and only one — situation in which the parties in a conflict are in the best position to solve it: the situation where resolution of the conflict is going to be through the exercise of sheer force. In every other situation the parties are at a disadvantage.

TENSION OF HOSTILITY

Two teams are having a tug of war across a fast-flowing river. The rope is wet so they have tied their bodies to the rope to get the best possible grip. Each team is pulling as hard as possible. For the moment the rope is stationary as force equals force. A great deal of effort is being exerted but there is no movement.

Neither side dares relax the tension because that side would immediately be dragged into the river. There is no communication between the sides. Even if there was communication there would be no trust. If one side suggested relaxing the tension the other side would regard this as a trick. There is a tension of hostility.

Two soft drink companies are spending a huge amount of money advertising their drinks. Each company knows that this huge expenditure is not increasing the market for the drinks. But neither side dare let up on the expenditure for a moment because the other company would immediately gain market share — which would be extremely expensive to recover. There is a tension of 'hostility'. Even though both sides recognize the waste of money and effort they dare not relax for a moment.

The arms race is a parallel example.

Conflict in general is characterized by this tension of hostility. There is constant pressure. A military commander dare not relax for a moment or the enemy will attack. A boxer dare not drop his guard.

Because of this tension of hostility it is extremely difficult for a party in a dispute to undertake the exploratory and provocative type of thinking that is essential for the design process. There cannot be the give and take needed to design an outcome because the basic principle is that nothing must be given unless its surrender has been forced.

This unfortunate situation has nothing to do with the good will of the people involved — or their good sense. They are all acting in a highly intelligent manner according to their logic bubbles. It is the logic of the situation that demands this behavior. The members of the two tug-of-war teams might dearly like to stop to have a beer and do some fishing in the river.

SECRECY, SUSPICION AND MISTRUST

This is a direct part of the tension of hostility. We can imagine the captain of one of the tug-of-war teams yelling across the river:

'I shall count up to three and then say STOP. At that moment we shall all relax tension.'

The other team would suspect that if they relaxed tension on the count of three they might immediately find themselves in the river.

It is natural to suppose that at every moment the other side is going to do something to gain an advantage. This is the perceptual context, and mood, in which any act is seen.

The days of chivalry in conflict and the Queensberry rules in fist fights are long gone. All is known to be fair in love and war.

In the Falklands War there were frantic efforts at negotiation through the Secretary General of the United Nations, through the President of Peru, through Alexander Haig, etc. Throughout these negotiations the British Government was conscious that time was passing and winter was coming on in the South Atlantic. The weather was getting worse and soon it might get too bad for the naval task force to mount an invasion of the Islands. So no matter how genuine the negotiation attempts might have been, they were always treated with suspicion as an attempt to gain a military advantage. So long as they could be seen in this way it does not matter whether this was or was not the case.

Psychological moves are an intrinsic part of normal conflict behavior. In the Second World War the Germans were misled into expecting the Allied landings in Normandy at quite the wrong beach. This misinformation led to their massing troops at the wrong place. It saved a large number of lives.

It is hardly surprising that secrecy has been an essential part of diplomacy and negotiation as well as part of conflict itself. Without secrecy there cannot be deception and there cannot be bluff.

As I mentioned before, we are guilty of *carrying over the idiom of conflict itself into our thinking about conflict*. Our conflict thinking has just been a miniature of the conflict that might actually take place on a battlefield. So secrecy and bluff has been essential.

A well-known businessman who had just concluded a brilliant deal to buy up a certain corporation told me:

> 'I wanted that organization very badly. If they had asked twice
> the price I would have paid it. But they didn't. So I got it cheap.'

Is it surprising that secrecy is a normal part of our negotiating? If the man had declared his best available price he would have had to pay double for the deal. What poker player wants to play with all his cards face up on the table? What would be the point of contract bridge if all hands were exposed at the start? Yet the chess pieces are visible enough on the board. Is there some significance in the fact that Russians play chess and the Americans play bridge and poker?

If one party knows that it is prepared to give something away in the negotiation then it does not want to give that away 'for free'. The maximum price must be extracted in return.

We take such secrecy for granted because it is an essential part of our current idiom of conflict thinking. We could not operate the present idiom without it. In the new 'design idiom', however, there can be much more openness since desires and fears all need to be stated so that they can become design ingredients. The parties involved in the conflict will clearly not make such disclosures to each other. So we see the essential role of the third party in the process.

LACK OF COMMUNICATION

Secrecy is, of course, a lack of communication. But what I want to mention here is the simple *absence* of a channel of communication between the parties in a conflict.

Between the end of the Falkland hostilities in 1982 and June 1984 there was no direct contact at all between the governments of Great Britain and Argentina. This is a childish absurdity. In a later section I shall discuss the absurdity of nations behaving like teenagers: sulks, taking offense, cold shoulders, not talking to each other, etc.

It is also an absurdity that warring nations do not talk to each other on a permanent basis *throughout the conflict.*

One of the roles for the organization I shall be describing later in this book (S.I.T.O.: Supranational Independent Thinking Organisation) will be to provide a forum for conflicting parties to be in permanent communication with each other — on a daily face-to-face basis.

I also believe there should be a permanent U.S.A./U.S.S.R. Council (possibly under the auspices of S.I.T.O.) rather than periodic meetings and walk-outs.

I do not want to go deeply into such matters here. I simply want to point out that, traditionally, the parties in a conflict often lack any direct communication with each other. This is yet another reason why there has to be a third party.

POSITION TAKING

In the bygone days of battle, commanders used to mark their position on the battlefield by means of their standards. These fluttering banners indicated to all who held what territory. These banners marked the positions reached at any moment. They showed achievement. They had a psychological value in showing the troops what was happening. They also had a very practical value in regrouping the scattered troops so that they knew where to rally and what points to defend.

Exactly the same thing happens in modern disputes. The leaders taking part need to signal to their supporters what is happening. They do this by means of banner statements. It would be quite impossible to describe in detail what is actually going on, so a few crisp slogans are used instead. Arthur Scargill, the miners' leader in Great Britain, declares that 'not one pit will be closed'. The Russians declare that there can be 'no further disarmament talks until the Cruise missiles are withdrawn'. This is traditional position taking. It indicates both where things are at and also the positions that are to be defended.

Unfortunately, a position taken in this public and defined a manner is extremely difficult to back out of. Negotiators are always 'painting themselves into corners' because of this need to show that the battle is being fought.

There is a dilemma of communication that occurs in many other areas. The dilemma arises from the need to communicate to two different groups at the same time.

In its annual report a corporation shows how very well things are going. This is essential in order to retain investor confidence, to maintain a good stock market quotation and to retain a good enough credit rating to make borrowing money easier. Indeed, the more a corporation needs to raise money the rosier the picture it is going to have to show to investors. Of course, the annual report is read by the workers and their union officials. If things are so rosy then surely that delayed wage rise should come through at this point? The demand for higher wages then makes life even more impossible for the corporation that is already short of money. With a message that is inevitably going to be visible to both groups, it is impossible to signal to investors that all is well and to workers that things are so bad that they must tighten their belts.

Exactly the same thing happens in conflicts. A leader has to signal a position in order to maintain the support of his or her followers. At the same time this rigid position makes negotiation much more difficult. There is another aspect of the same phenomenon with national insult trading. For the sake of his home supporters a leader may have to appear belligerent. At the same time he may well wish to cool matters down as regards the other power involved. So he has to offer fierce insults and somehow simultaneously convey that these are only for 'home consumption'. The excellence of modern communication makes this task increasingly difficult. What might have been said to a rally of political supporters is now immediately available to the rest of the world.

Because position taking is always accompanied by such suitable noises as 'never yield', 'resist to the death' and 'no change in our position', the parties involved in the dispute are never in the best position to explore the adjustments needed in order to design an outcome.

There is yet another aspect of public position taking. This is the 'ritual dance'. It often happens in union negotiations that both sides are shrewd and experienced enough to know what the outcome is going to be. The matter could almost be decided at the first meeting. In most countries (other than Japan) this cannot be done. There is a traditional way of doing things: the ritual dance. There have to be excessive demands and threats and the breaking off of talks and the rest. All this is necessary for two reasons.

If there is no ritual dance then union members will never believe that their officials have done their job properly. The officials will be seen as weak and too ready to compromise. At next election time such 'weak' officials will be replaced by tougher ones.

The second reason is that the officials themselves cannot know they have got the best possible bargain unless they exert the maximum possible pressure each time. It is rather like the businessman who got the corporation cheap because the other side did not demand the highest possible price. There always has to be both a good case and 'maximum possible pressure'. If you are seen to exert maximum possible pressure then you show to your followers — and to yourself — that you simply have got the best bargain possible. How else could you show it?

LABELS

At various points in the book I have mentioned the problem of language and labels. Here I am concerned with stock insults.

If the opposing side is an 'enemy' and 'evil' then constructive talks are more difficult. If the other party is a 'bully' and 'aggressor' and a 'dictator' then even to be seen negotiating with that person is seen as a surrender of sorts.

Such labels are necessary in order to stoke up support for a cause and to enhance the righteousness of one's case. They are also good for stirring speeches. Newspapers love them and imaginatively display a variety of such labels in clever headlines.

We have here the dilemma of 'public consumption' and 'negotiating consumption' that I mentioned earlier in this section.

It should also be remembered that there is another purpose behind these insults. They can serve to set the 'mood' of the negotiation. As I explained in an earlier section, a tough or obdurate mood may actually alter the concepts available to the other party. In other words, there is good reason to 'browbeat' an opponent.

ENJOYMENT

There is an attraction and an enjoyment in conflict and crises. Politicians often love crises. This is in addition to the use of a conflict in order to rally support for an unpopular regime and to unite quarreling factions by pinpointing an external enemy (or an internal one in the case of the Jews in Nazi Germany).

A crisis or a conflict focuses the minds of politicians. Many politicians are 'reactor' thinkers. They are much happier reacting to something than taking the initiative in improving society through imaginative action. They are simply not creative and not designers. Besides, any initiative is risky since it may not work and may upset as many people as it benefits. Reaction thinking is much safer. You only do what you are forced to do. Any action — or even survival itself — is an immense achievement. Even 'not giving way' on a point becomes a triumph.

Because of this attractiveness and political utility of a conflict, the parties involved may not be the most motivated to solve that conflict. So they will not seek creative or designed outcomes for fear that, once made visible, such a suggestion could make the conflict difficult to continue. If there is an obvious solution it becomes difficult to pretend it does not exist.

TWO-FINGER TYPING

The world is full of skilled and experienced negotiators in unions, in governments, in diplomatic services, in the United Nations and in law offices. Surely such people are better placed than anyone else to solve conflicts. Surely the skilled negotiators available within the ranks of the parties involved in a conflict are in the best position to solve that conflict through direct negotiation with the other side.

Not so. Even if they think so.

Busy journalists spend much of their life typing. They have great experience of typewriters and keyboards. But many of them go through life *typing with two index fingers*. They peck away at the keyboard in a remarkably inefficient manner when compared with a junior office typist who has only a few months experience but has acquired the skill of touch typing with all fingers.

Using a bad skill very efficiently does not make it a good skill. Practicing a bad skill over years of experience still leaves it as a bad skill.

A tennis player or a golfer may have an inherent style fault which he or she is totally unable to correct. It needs an outside coach to come along to point out the fault and to set about correcting it. Practicing harder without such fault correction will only embed the fault even more.

So experienced conflict participants or skilled negotiators or skilled dialecticians may only be skillful at the old conflict idioms of argument. They may have no skill at all with the design idiom. Skill and experience are simply not sufficient unless we say at what.

Let us be quite clear that experience in a situation may build up a sensitivity to that situation but does not necessarily ever develop the best way of dealing with it. Half an hour in a medical classroom may give better instruction on how to deal with a drowned person than twenty years of pulling people out of the sea (without any instruction).

It is a fatal mistake to assume that experience is the same as skill. It is a fatal mistake to assume that if a skill is used it must be the right skill. It is most useful to keep in mind the metaphor of the two-finger typists.

All those people who have built up skill in the old idiom of conflict thinking — where the thinking is an extension of the conflict — should not assume that that is the only or the best approach to conflict resolution. If we are content to leave conflict resolution to such people then this assumption will be made. And we shall remain stuck for ever within an idiom that has shown itself to be inadequate.

OUTSIDE VIEW

We come now to the final reason why the parties involved in a conflict may be in the worst position to resolve that conflict. It has to do with perception.

In an earlier section I mentioned that, in the scientific method, once the 'most reasonable' hypothesis had been formed it became very difficult to see the evidence in any other way. This is because of the way perception works as a self-organizing system. Evidence is not placed neutrally on a 'passive' information surface but exists in the 'active' self-organizing environment of perception.

Exactly the same thing happens with conflicts. Each of the parties has a position. That position dominates perception and organizes the elements of the situation to support the position. The elements are simply not available for designing into a new structure because such a structure would at once seem inferior to the chosen position. This is not a fault of the people involved or evidence of their bigoted attitude. It simply follows from the logic of patterning systems.

In a perceptual sense you cannot haul yourself up 'by your bootstraps'.

I shall return to this point later when I deal specifically with the third party role in conflict resolution. It is a fundamental point.

There is also a related but different point. If you are too closely involved in a situation it is difficult to get an *overview* or to get a sense of *perspective*. That is another reason why those involved are not in the best position to resolve the conflict. As you pursue one road you may not be in a helicopter position to survey alternative roads.

SUMMARY

What I have tried to show in this section is that the parties involved in a conflict may actually be in the worst position to resolve that conflict —except where the outcome is to be determined by force. I want to emphasize that I do not consider this due to ill will or greed on the part of those involved. It is the logic of the situation and it could not be otherwise. To expect from a combatant the heroics of complete disclosure and complete faith in the other party is to expect stupidity.

It is true that there are habits of thinking and habits of conflict behavior (like calling each other names) which are not strictly necessary and which do make conflict resolution more difficult. We could improve thinking styles and get rid of the worst habits and that would improve matters considerably. Nevertheless, the very involvement of the parties and the fact that they have much to gain or to lose makes them incapable of providing all the thinking needed for resolution of the conflict.

This inevitable thinking inadequacy of the disputants in a dispute creates a dilemma. It is natural for the disputants to consider a dispute to be their business alone. In the complexity of the modern world, where everything affects everything else, this is rarely so and disputes tend to have a harmful effect on all those around. In spite of this, those involved in a quarrel feel it is their business to sort it out. This is because sorting it out is always conceived on a 'trial of strength' basis and the intrusion of others would unfairly alter the balance of strength. So the combatants are incapable of designing their way out of a conflict and yet are reluctant to have anyone else involved. This reluctance is a dangerous arrogance because for the design approach to work there has to be 'triangular thinking' and the involvement of a third party, for the reasons I have spelled out in this section.

CHAPTER 11

CONTINUITY

In this section I am going to consider the dangers of continuity and how we are imprisoned by the sequence of experience that makes up our personal, cultural or national past. The past is not a series of books on a library shelf so placed that we can, at leisure, pick a lesson from history. The past is our language, concepts, thinking habits, attitudes and social structures. At various points in this book I have commented on the dangerous way in which language is a cumulative record of our culture: dangerous because it forces us to follow concepts which are no longer valid. Language is an encyclopedia of ignorance. A concept enters language at a state of relative ignorance. Thereafter it is frozen into permanence by some word.

Because I am going to be writing about the dangers of continuity I must make clear at the outset that there is a great deal of good that can be written in favor of continuity. Quite simply, life and civilization would be utterly impossible without continuity. Just as perception would be impossible without the rigid patterns that have formed, so the organization of life would be impossible without the behavioral patterns that have formed. In both cases we can look at the dangers of such rigid patterns provided we also acknowledge their immense value.

Foreign affairs can hardly work at all if treaties mean nothing and promises cannot be relied upon. Since any agreement tends to be about something that is going to happen (or not happen) in the future there has to be continuity. There is a very disturbing tendency in modern conflict thinking to talk about 'new situations'.

The Japanese contracted a very favorable long-term sugar contract with Australia. The price of sugar then fell dramatically so that what the Japanese had been getting at half market prices suddenly turned out to be double market prices. They refused to honor the contract and claimed that there was a 'new situation' and the contract should be renegotiated. They said that in Japanese culture a contract was only an intention to do business on a mutually advantageous basis and if circumstances changed the contract needed changing too. The Australian Government thought differently.

When the Alfonsin Government replaced the military junta in Argentina there was some reluctance to honor the large debts run up by the previous regime (since it was not democratic). Revolutionary Red Russia declined to honor the Czarist bonds of the government that had been overthrown.

It is obvious that debts, promises and treaties all become worthless if a party can plead 'new situation' and cancel the continuity of any commitment. In a negotiating situation one side may put an offer on the table. Later that offer may be withdrawn because of a 'new situation'.

In the old days of diplomacy promises had to be kept otherwise a nation would lose its credibility. This was equivalent to a nation losing its credit rating with the banks. No one would deal with that nation. Today there is more pragmatic tolerance and a feeling that a new regime has a right to a fresh start.

The Russian foreign affairs department has remarkable continuity. The same man may sit at the West German desk for twenty or thirty years. He knows intimately what is going on in the country. This may be contrasted with the complete lack of continuity in American politics and the foreign service where an ambassador to an important country will change with the new administration and may be someone with no foreign service experience at all — let alone experience with that country. On the one hand the Russian continuity gives the great advantages of experience and understanding. On the other hand that continuity can lock in a person's thinking. So continuity has advantages and disadvantages.

In this section I shall be writing about the disadvantages.

MOMENT TO MOMENT

In a previous section I wrote about the 'tension of hostility' and used the image of two tug-of-war teams, neither of which dared relax the tension for a moment. In Northern Ireland none of the parties involved dares relax its hostility towards the other parties for a single moment because at that moment the party would instantly be condemned by its supporters as having 'gone soft'.

In the resolution of any conflict this moment-to-moment continuity is most important. When is the 'break' going to come? How are steadfast positions ever going to be abandoned? It is just possible to conceive of a position being exchanged for another equally advantageous position but it is very difficult for a position to be abandoned so that the first tentative steps of exploration can be made towards a designed outcome.

'I am locked in. What can I do?'

That is a common plea of any negotiator.

The solution is for the third party (in triangular thinking) to make the break with continuity whilst the parties apparently hold fast to their positions.

THE EDGE EFFECT

This is a concept I introduced in my book 'Future Positive' (published by Penguin Books Ltd., London). It means that there may be a wonderful destination but if we are unable to take the first step then the wonders of the destination are pointless. The edge effect follows directly from moment-to-moment continuity.

In the end an agreement between the U.K. and Argentina will have to be reached. But any suggestion that the sovereignty of the Islands might even be discussed has a very negative effect because of the lives lost in retaking the Islands (which would then seem to have been lost in vain).

In the business world it is quite common for an idea to have an initial 'negative cash flow'. That means that a lot of money will have to be spent before an idea starts to become profitable. It is expected that an idea may be negative at first. But in almost any other situation it is not possible to work with 'negative cash flow' ideas. The offered idea has to be attractive at once. Even if a leader in a conflict saw the ultimate value of an idea that was negative at first, that leader would have a hard time taking his followers with him.

There are also the idioms of 'thin end of the wedge' and 'domino effect'. Both these idioms imply that some minor concession is actually very important because it is then going to lead inevitably to something very serious. Once the first step has been conceded it may be impossible to halt the slide. Such idioms make even more difficult the use of ideas with an initial negative cash flow.

Revolutionaries have always felt that revolution is essential because society will never be willing to take the small transitional steps required to make it more equitable. Each step, no matter how small, will always be perceived by those in power as having a negative effect and will be fiercely resisted. So peaceful change becomes impossible.

TRANSITIONAL STEPS

It is clear that the design of an outcome to a conflict has to pay a great deal of attention to the transitional steps. It is not just a matter of designing a satisfactory outcome. Each step of the way to that outcome has to be designed. The very first step is the most important of all. These transitional steps may be the most important part of the design task. These are the steps that are going to break the moment-to-moment continuity.

It is very important that the first step should not have a negative aspect to it. It is extremely valuable if the first step can have a positive appeal.

You can push a steel ball along a surface with your finger. If the surface is a sponge mat you can propel the ball without ever touching it. With your finger you depress the sponge just ahead of the ball. The balls rolls into the depression. So by creating an area of 'attraction' ahead of the ball you can lead it wherever you wish. That is the obvious value of transitional steps with appeal. The payment of attractive redundancy money to workers who are being laid off is an example.

CONDITIONS AT THE TIME

We can now move away from moment-to-moment continuity in order to consider the long-term effects of continuity.

Many countries run a 'respresentative' type of democracy. In an election the voters choose someone who is going to represent them in parliament or congress. The idea is that this representative should think, talk and vote on behalf of the people who voted for him or her. This essential basis of democracy depended on the conditions of the time. When communication was poor it was clearly necessary to have a 'representative' who could travel to the center of power to represent the views of other people who had to stay at home. Today we have remarkable communication systems: there is even interactive television so that a viewer at home can press a button on the set and 'vote' on any issue presented on the screen. Our techniques of opinion polling are very sophisticated. By testing a cross-section sample it is possible to obtain from less than 2,000 people a view that might represent millions.

The point is that modern technology will certainly open up the possibility of 'direct democracy' so that people will be able to vote directly on issues instead of via their chosen representative. To some extent this happens in Switzerland where the small cantonal system has always permitted direct referenda on all possible matters. Of course the 'leadership' quality of democracy will be lost. This implies that the chosen representative will not just reflect the views of his electors but will actually improve upon them (this is but a hope).

Many things come about in a certain way because the conditions and technology of the time determined that particular way. Continuity then keeps things going in that same way — even though it is no longer necessary.

THE RATCHET EFFECT

There was a time when steam trains required stokers. Under these conditions agreement was reached between union and managers as to the number of men required on the footplate. With the advent of electric locomotives, stokers were no longer required. But the unions still insisted on having the same number of men on the footplate — in order to preserve jobs. The same thing happened in Fleet Street, in London. Improvements in printing technology meant that fewer workers were needed. The unions extracted agreements to maintain ghost crews who were paid to do work that no longer existed. These are perfectly reasonable actions that fit with the logic bubbles of the union negotiators. These are examples of continuity based on past conditions.

The ratchet effect describes how we may be willing enough to take an 'upward step' but extremely reluctant ever to give up an advantage once gained. It applies to people's life styles and expectations. An increase in income leads to an improvement in standard of living. Soon this becomes a standard expectation. Any attempt to reduce that standard is met with fierce opposition.

Advantages offered on a temporary basis cannot later be taken away without much fuss. A frequent bonus for good work becomes an expected part of salary.

The important point is that a great deal of fuss may be made about giving up things to which there is no real right at all. This is an important consideration for conflict thinking.

A worker who has got into the habit of giving a colleague a ride to work finds that an enemy has been created when the rides stop.

ZERO BASE

Each advance is based on where you are at the moment. Business corporations easily lose direction: they are set up to serve a market need, but when they reach a certain size their momentum is related no longer to the market need but to the current shape of the organization.

If a senior executive dining room has come into being, then at budget time a budget is allocated for that purpose. The concept of 'zero base' budgeting is that nothing is taken for granted. The base is supposed to revert to zero. Instead of calculating the budget needed for the senior executive dining room a review is made to see whether such a dining room is needed at all. The idea is excellent, but in practice the continuity of existing structures often insures that a reasonable defense can be made for most existing structures.

Much as we might like to get back to zero basics, our next step is very much determined by where we are at the moment. This is obvious in conflict situations where a desire to clear the board, forget about the past and get down to the basics of the situation is an attractive intention — but very difficult to carry out.

I would love to do some zero-base thinking on language and the concepts it makes available. But that is never going to be possible. Nor is there much hope for zero-basic thinking on various institutions and structures in society.

APOSTOLIC SUCCESSION

The Catholic Church believes that the Protestant bishops are not real bishops because there has been a loss of the 'Apostolic Succession'. This means a loss of the continuity whereby the apostle Peter appointed bishops who in turn appointed bishops and so on in a continuous succession that was broken when different churches broke away from Rome.

In practice the Apostolic Succession means that the people doing the selection for an organization always choose people in their own image. In turn these selected people do likewise. So the culture of an institution becomes permanently frozen. It happens in universities all the time. It happens with all public services and all bureaucratic organizations. It happens with newspapers.

It happens with political parties for those chosen are those who best reflect existing thinking and attitudes.

In conflicts it means that those involved in thinking about the conflict are those most likely to reflect the old and traditional thinking about that conflict. In organizations like the United Nations it means that the staff are most likely to reflect the traditional thinking of the organization. In this way issues and organizations tend to get ever more frozen into their molds.

RICOCHET

The ricochet type of continuity has two parts. An institution is set up to facilitate a certain activity. The institution carries out this function and gets stronger. Finally the institution does not merely facilitate the activity but actually determines what can be done.

A prime example is the banking system. Gold was left with goldsmiths who had the means for storing and protecting it. The owner was given a 'certificate of ownership'. This certificate became his means for settling debts. So long as everyone knew that the gold was there should it be required, then it was possible to extend credit and create capital. The banks made all this possible. In the end the banks had achieved such a dominant position that they now determine the nature of much financial activity.

School systems set up examination boards to facilitate their work. Before long the examination boards become all-powerful and now dictate to the schools what they should be doing.

Representative organizations set up to settle conflicts eventually become polarized into power blocs and alliances and then only serve to exacerbate conflicts.

NEGLECT

For about forty years the driver of a motor car would indicate an intention to change direction with a trafficator arm which would rise from the side of the vehicle. This was a most inefficient system since it was invisible from many angles and it was always sticking or being broken off. In fact it was a direct remnant of the way a coachman would hold out his whip to indicate a direction change — or a driver in earlier open cars would hold out an arm.

It was only forty years later that there was a change to the much more effective flashing light system — which had been technically possible all along.

We are so oriented towards 'problem-solving' that if something is not actually a problem it gets very little thinking time. So something continues unchallenged simply because no one has ever thought to challenge a particular assumption.

COMPLACENCY

This type of continuity is related to 'neglect' but refers to an idea which has worked very well in the past. We come to believe that an idea which has worked well on repeated occasions is an absolutely valid idea. When it ceases to work well we do not challenge the continued relevance of that idea.

Instead we blame special circumstances, interfering factors, wrong attitudes or the incompetence of the people involved. We do not challenge the concept itself. We think that because it has worked in the past there cannot be any fault in the concept.

I believe that we are extremely complacent about our thinking styles and about many institutions. They have worked well in the past so we tend to think that any shortfall is not due to the system itself but only to the way it happens to be operated at the moment. I think this is quite wrong — as I have pointed out throughout this book.

As I shall point out later, I believe that the United Nations itself is a case in point. Because we are complacent about that organization we may ignore the need to set up another organization better designed for conflict resolution.

TIME SEQUENCE

In a way this summarizes all the different aspects of continuity. Things happen over time. A coming together of things at a particular time forms a structure or a concept. Once this exists then it can be added to. But the intrinsic elements are no longer free to come together in a new way.

The reason we always treat sick people in hospital is that in the Middle Ages the most caring groups in society were the religious orders of monks and nuns. They lived in enclosed communities. So it was natural for sick people to be brought to these communities. Thus the structure and the concept of a hospital developed, and it has stayed with us to dominate our concept of the delivery of health care. There are advantages in terms of the need to centralize expensive equipment and very specialized care, but there is no reason to suppose that hospitals are the best way of delivering about 80% of health care. This might well be done better in small units.

Similarly many of our concepts of war and conflict are determined by a particular sequence of history. Our conflict concepts are not far removed from those of a king leading his warriors into battle. For example, there need not be homogeneity in a conflict resolution. There need not be an outcome which is satisfactory to all on one side. There could be different solutions for different factions — and even a different negotiating team.

When I am teaching I often hand out a few shapes and ask people to assemble these shapes to give a simple figure. The shapes are placed together to form a rectangle. I offer further shapes. The rectangle is extended to give a bigger rectangle. I offer more shapes and now there is a problem. The new pieces cannot be added to the existing rectangle to give a coherent shape.

The only way forward is to go back and to dismantle what was a 'correct' arrangement at the time in order to free up the pieces so that all the pieces can now be put together. The result is a simple square.

The principle illustrated in this fashion is simple: elements can get imprisoned in a particular structure and progress may depend on freeing them up in order to create a better structure that takes advantage of later-arriving elements.

Whether we like it or not, we have to admit that we are inevitably trapped by continuity. We could put it in the form of a rather startling axiom:

'No idea could ever make the best use of its ingredients.'

This is because the ingredients will have arrived over time and so the development of the idea will be time dependent. Yet the best arrangement should be time independent — as if all the pieces had appeared simultaneously. They could never appear simultaneously because if they did we should be unable to understand them.

An appreciation of this axiom is very motivating for the exercise of creativity. It means that locked up in our concepts and structures are elements which could be freed to form better and more relevant designs.

SUMMARY

Our thinking habits lead us to believe that if you are careful and 'right' at each step then progress will be made by steps forward.

This is a fallacy. A consideration of continuity will show that in order to move forward we may actually have to move back and dismantle a concept or structure that was valid in its time. If we refuse this notion then we select revolution as the only possible method of change. We also select conflict and dialectic clash.

It is unfortunate that with conflict there are set concepts, set structures and set positions. The tension of hostility creates a moment-to-moment continuity that cannot be broken.

For anyone involved in conflict thinking a very good understanding of the logic and mechanics of continuity is absolutely essential.

We need to know how we are trapped by continuity — because this is an unnecessary trap. It is a trap in which we do not have to remain if we have the wit to know we are in a trap.

CHAPTER 12

OBJECTIVES, BENEFITS AND VALUES

An objective is something that you set out to achieve. It is something towards which you aim your efforts. An objective can be defined. You believe an objective to be within your reach (it may or may not be in fact). You take steps to reach your objective. You make action decisions depending on whether the action is going to advance you to your objective. There may be sub-objectives which you aim to reach on the way to the final objective. It is to be hoped that you have a clear idea of your objective.

A benefit is something that flows from the achieved objective. A benefit is something that affects you in a beneficial way. The benefit is a benefit because it delivers some value. A benefit can be measured in an objective way — a value cannot. The reason you aim for the objective is that you believe it will deliver benefits once you get there. Benefits do not always have to be earned. They can be granted or even stumbled upon.

A value is what is delivered by a benefit. A value is a way of looking at something. One man isolated in a hut on a deserted island may value the peace and natural environment. Another man might hate the boredom. One man may welcome the organized routine and predictability of an army life. Another man may find it oppressive and restricting. Value, like beauty, is in the eye of the beholder. Like beauty there are some types of value which are readily visible to most people. Values are not always obvious and there may be a special way of looking at something which suddenly reveals a value. At a meeting in New Zealand all the executives present complained about the heavy government control on industry. One person welcomed this regulation and claimed that it held back his competitors very nicely. Values and needs go together. Food is especially valuable when you are hungry. Freedom is especially valuable when you are not free.

We tend to think of conflicts in terms of an aggressor and a victim. The aggressor is the party who sets the conflict in motion. We tend to think that the aggressor has a certain objective to be reached and the victim's objective is to resist the aggressor. This is the simplistic and moralistic view of a conflict. The aggressor is in the wrong and must be resisted. It may be that the aggressor's objective will offer special benefits to him. Perhaps this objective does not disadvantage the victim. Perhaps there are even benefits for the 'victim'. Perhaps a way can be found to align the interests of aggressor and victim. In any case we need to look beyond the simple label of 'aggressor'. We also need to look beyond the first stated objectives. It may be that there are other ways of obtaining the same benefits.

When we get away from the aggressor/victim conflict model we find a genuine clash of interests. The two parties want things which are incompatible. One half of the town wants to bring in a rubber factory to provide employment. The other half wants to keep out the smelly factory because it will spoil the environment. The clash of interest is at the objective level: bring in the factory or do not bring in the factory. At the benefit level there is delivery of employment and delivery of smell. The ultimate values are employment and environmental. There might be a way of making a rubber factory non-smelly. There might be a way of providing employment with a different sort of factory. The main objectors might be invited to become shareholders in the factory with special 'inconvenience shares'. The factory might be located a little bit further out of town and a transport system provided.

A basic design technique is to move away from the obvious clash point and to explore benefits and values in various modifications of the situation.

The creation of benefits requires some actual adjustment to the situation. The creation of values may only require a perceptual adjustment.

For example, a hidden value factor for the objectors to the factory might · have been a fear that the price of their houses would go down because of the smell in the district. Another way of looking at it might be that employment in the area would create a demand for houses and that unemployment would make houses difficult to sell.

TIME SCALE

A con-man always sells values for future delivery. The larger the promise the more likely are people to believe that the value will ultimately be delivered. They want to believe it so they do.

Future values are an important part of the design of conflict outcomes. Each side needs to be sure that it is not left in a vulnerable position. Each side would like to believe that, even if present benefits are not much, there is the chance for greater future benefits. The German metalworkers' union settled for a 38½-hour week but part of the agreement was that in future individual plants might make their own arrangements. This might allow the union to use a creep strategy in which those plants who could best afford it would reduce the working week — to be followed by the others later.

A change in principle might offer no immediate benefit but can offer a future value.

Any investment is an acceptance of cash deprivation at the moment in order to receive back increased cash in the future. In a conflict situation, if different parties have different confidence in the future then it becomes possible to offer future values to one party in exchange for present values to the other. These values would be delivered by specific benefits written into the agreement. It is not enough just to offer the hope that the future will deliver the value; there has to be some way of formulating a benefit. For example, a stock option is a real benefit whereas the hope that the corporate stock will rise is no offered benefit.

Staged benefits simply mean that the benefits will be phased over time. They are promised and there is no risk attached. It can, of course, happen that if circumstances change the value of the benefits may also change. Index linking would protect monetary values against inflation but there can be other changes of circumstance.

CONDITIONAL BENEFITS

If 'something' happens then 'something else' will happen. Conditional benefits are used to allay fears. If the volume of traffic through the airport reaches a certain level then a night curfew will be imposed. It may be unrealistic and too expensive to allay all possible fears at the time of designing a conflict outcome. Conditional clauses can be very valuable in this regard.

There is another type of conditional clause which states that some benefit will be given provided performance has reached a certain level. This is typical of productivity agreements. Such clauses protect a party against empty promises. They also reward special effort.

MATCHED BENEFITS

This is a sort of auction of good intentions. One party offers to do something if the other party will match it. In a sense it is a conditional benefit but the only condition is that the other party is willing to behave in a similar way: we will refrain from issuing bulletins on this problem if you also refrain; we will trade the prisoners we hold for the ones you hold. The auction aspect is if one side is willing to go higher than the other side. We will offer so much: can you match that? This aspect of conflict outcomes is, to my mind, insufficiently used, probably because we regard conflict resolution as a matter of compromise within demanded benefits rather than the creation of new benefits to open up opportunity pathways. After all the whole concept of judo is to open up new opportunity pathways for the offered force.

JOINT BENEFITS

Here the two parties actually come together in a joint venture that will produce benefits for both of them. Instead of being antagonistic they are now partners in this limited regard. It is not uncommon in real estate development for the developers to join with the planning authority so that the developers get what they want but in turn the planners get something they could not have had before. As I mentioned above, the whole negative attitude towards conflict (we are right and they are wrong) is extremely inhibitory when it comes to designing benefits into the outcome. The attitude is still one of 'how much can we get away with' and 'how little are we forced to give up'.

REWARDS

In the concept of 'greenmail' in the U.S.A. a corporate raider buys up shares in a corporation and threatens a takeover. In the end, in order to rid itself of this threat, the corporation may buy back these shares at a substantial premium. It is a form of blackmail with dollars (greenbacks), hence the term 'greenmail'. The concept of 'blackmail' is a real one and we do have to be very cautious in its vicinity. Nevertheless we must not let this concept block any attempt to design rewards into a conflict outcome. We must not assume that every conflict is an aggressor's attempt to see 'what he can get away with'.

CHAPTER 13

CREATIVITY

C reativity is a key part of the design process and is therefore an essential ingredient in the 'designed outcome' approach to conflict resolution. An understanding of the principles — and logical basis — of creativity is absolutely necessary for anyone who is going to be involved in the design approach to conflicts. Unfortunately the idioms of creative thinking are most at variance with the idioms of dialectic argument. For this reason the people normally involved in conflict resolution are the least likely to be able to provide the creative input. It is not just a matter of talent or temperament; the role of the disputants is such that the provocations and speculations of creativity are simply not open to them. Hence the need for the third party in triangular thinking.

There is a great deal of rubbish written about creativity because — like motherhood — it is automatically a good thing. My preference is to treat creativity as a logical process rather than a matter of talent or mystique.

If we look at the information universe of 'active' self-organizing information systems we begin to understand the logic of such systems. For this we can see the essential need for lateral thinking and we can also design effective practical tools which can be used in a deliberate manner.

I invented the term 'lateral thinking' many years ago because the term 'creativity' is too general, too vague, too full of artistic connotations and too value laden. Indeed, many creative people are not creative at all. Some artists are no more than productive stylists inasmuch as they produce within a defined style. Some creative people are also very rigid. They may have an unusual, and valuable, idea but remain rigidly within that idea. This is often seen in research departments where 'creative scientists' may be very rigid in their thinking. It is also very common in advertising agencies.

Lateral thinking is specifically concerned with the ability to escape from existing perceptual (and conceptual) patterns in order to open up new ways of looking at things and doing things. The word is now officially part of the English language with an entry in the Oxford English Dictionary, which decides such matters. Throughout this book I have used the word 'creativity' because most readers may not yet be familiar with the term lateral thinking.

THE FIRST FLYING MACHINE

Why were the Wright brothers the first men to fly? They did not start off with any new technology that was not available to others. They succeeded because they changed the basic concept — they succeeded because they used 'lateral thinking'.

All those working to design flying machines would make small models which they would launch through the air. Since such models had to fly on their own they had to be stable. So the design direction was towards designing *stable aircraft*. Each little advance was a step forward in this direction. The Wright brothers came along and changed the concept. They decided to design *unstable* aircraft. This set their thinking going in a new direction.

In an unstable aircraft, if a wing dips then the plane will bank and crash. So there is a need to change the relative lift on the wings so as to level the plane out again. The Wright brothers found a way of doing this by warping or twisting the wings. So they developed controls and became the first to fly.

This story is a very interesting illustration of how it may be enough for lateral thinking to set a new *concept direction*. From that point on the direction may be pursued with logical, technical and experimental thinking which may, or may not, have a further creative input. This is a very important point because we often erroneously believe that the purpose of creativity is only to provide solutions. Often the most useful function of creativity is to set *new directions*. Once we start to think in these new directions then experience and concepts already available to us can be put together to produce the needed design. This point is highly relevant to conflict resolution because often the impasse is caused by the parties looking at the situation in rather a rigid way. The mere suggestion of a new approach may be enough to get thinking moving towards a resolution.

As a matter of interest, the same concept change effect was later seen with the design of the first airplane to be powered solely by a man's muscles. Many people had shown mathematically that such an airplane could never fly because man could not produce enough power. My good friend Paul MacCready succeeded and won the Kramer prize which had been around for a long time. Instead of designing such a machine — as everyone else had tried to do — he took an existing lightweight flying machine and worked from that. So he used the hang-glider as a conceptual base.

There are three basic types of progress: technical progress, system progress and concept progress. I shall deal with each in turn.

TECHNICAL PROGRESS

With technical progress we are going along and then some new technical development comes about. Immediately we fit that new development into what we are doing. We take advantage of it.

The jet engine comes along and we immediately put it into aircraft instead of the propeller engine. The transistor comes along and we immediately use it to replace the triode valve as our means of amplification in electronic systems: radios, television, computers, etc.

Technical progress is incredibly rapid because we are ready to use the new development. We can plug it in immediately. Progress is in effect geometric. There are no objectors apart from the manufacturers of the obsolete products.

Creativity is needed to appreciate the potential of the new development. Creativity is needed to fit it in and to maximize that potential. There is a lot of creativity still needed in order for us to make the best use of our computer and telecommunication technology. We have not even made full use of our television technology. We have only made use of the technology of weaponry to create the concept of mutual deterrence.

SYSTEM PROGRESS

System progress is much slower than technical progress. With system progress the 'elements' may be available and may have been lying around for a long time until someone *designs them* into a new concept. This type of progress is typical of design. There is no sudden technical input. It is a matter of someone setting out to put things together in a design — and succeeding.

From the availability of the elements to their incorporation as a design may take years or decades or even longer. It all depends on will and talent. It depends on the will of people to try to put together designs. It depends on the design talent of those who try.

It is exactly this type of progress that is required in the design approach to conflict resolution. How can the different elements (made available by Think-2 and mapping) be designed into an outcome?

A classic example of such system progress is the design of the European Common Market. The Red Cross itself and the Geneva Convention are other triumphs of design.

The important point is that there is nothing inevitable about system progress. We may remain stuck with an inefficient system simply because no one has set out to design a better one. It took years for the very simple 'one queue system' to get into banks, offices and airlines (everyone is in one queue and the person at the head of the queue goes to whichever serving position is vacant — as distinct from having a separate queue for each position and getting stuck behind a 'difficult' case).

CONCEPT PROGRESS

This is very slow indeed. It explains why we have made so much technical progress and so very little social progress. It explains why our weapon systems are so sophisticated and our conflict thinking so primitive.

This type of progress relates directly to self-organizing systems and some of the points I discussed in the section on continuity. Initial experience comes together to form a pattern or a structure. Once that exists it controls the way future experience is treated. The pattern reinforces itself and becomes stronger. As a perception it organizes future experience and as a structure it organizes society around itself. As we have already seen elsewhere in the book, the concepts that enter language then come to control our thinking.

Where progress depends on our being able to *backtrack* in order to escape from a pattern then progress will be very slow indeed. Our mind is simply not designed for that. Nor are our thinking habits. That is why we need specifically to develop lateral thinking which is designed for pattern changing.

WHY CONCEPT EVOLUTION IS NOT ENOUGH

If we do not believe in creativity then we have to rely on concept evolution. This means that existing concepts are continually being improved by new knowledge. A concept is regarded as a garden that can ever be improved by further attention. Progress is always forward from the existing version of the concept to a better version.

We might also believe that the pressure of events and changes in the environment will exert an evolutionary pressure on concepts. This pressure will mold the concepts and make them better. So union pressure on management will gradually improve the concept of capitalistic employment. The role of a thinker is to contribute to the pressures that will improve concepts. It is therefore enough to criticize and complain because this provides evolutionary pressure.

This is in fact what we do believe. A politician has the self-image of a driver in charge of a car. The car is moving forward. The road is tricky and winding. The driver's task is to steer the car sensitively and to keep it on the road. There is no question of choosing the car, the road or the destination, or even providing the motor power. All this is done by 'the natural course of events'. This means the myriad of changes that together form progress.

There are two serious limitations to this picture. The first is that there is no provision at all for backtracking and undoing a concept which is no longer relevant and which is blocking progress. Being right at each step is not enough. We may occasionally have to go back and take a different route. We find this extremely hard to do.

The second limitation is that progress may be very slow if we have to wait for evolution. All the elements may be available long before evolution forms them into a new concept. We can no longer afford this length of time since technological changes have become so rapid.

We must remember that there are many evolutionary blind alleys. Evolution may take a wrong turn. Evolution determined by a particular set of circumstances might end up as a wrong turn if the circumstances change. An animal evolved to lose heat rapidly would die out if the climate got cooler. Political systems designed for stable societies might be quite useless if times become unstable.

BLOCKING

We may regard a lack of creativity simply as an inability to design a better idea. But we should never forget that the existence of a current concept or institution may actually *block* the emergence of a better concept. The existence of the 'university' concept may block the emergence of a new type of whole-life education. When elements and resources are tied up in one way they are not free to be reassembled in a different way. The very concept of 'bargaining' makes it difficult to design better ways of determining wages. It is not just that the adequacy of a concept or the complacency with which it is held removes any design motivation — there is also the difficulty of escaping from the current pattern to see things differently.

The divide between capital and employment makes it difficult to conceive the idea that workers might own the robots in the factories instead of just being displaced by them.

The words 'workers' and 'employment' serve to fossilize concepts which need changing.

THE CREATIVITY DILEMMA

We come now to the reason why society has managed very well without paying too much attention to creativity outside the artistic area.

Every valuable creative idea will always be logical in hindsight.

I shall explain the reason for this in a moment. Since every valuable creative idea is logical in hindsight it is then supposed that what is needed is not creativity at all but just better logic. It follows that logic is the complete thinking system after all. This is a very serious fallacy which has held up the development of creativity.

As I explained in an earlier section, perception occurs in a self-organizing information system where incoming information forms itself into patterns. We can consider these as tracks or channels, since each particular state is followed inevitably by a subsequent state. If we enter the beginning of the pattern we proceed along to the end.

Consider now the possibility of side patterns like side roads off the main road. When we come to such a side pattern do we have to stop and consider which direction to follow? We should forever be dithering and there would be a need for another brain to do the deciding. In fact this is not necessary. The organization of nerve architecture is such that the dominant pattern suppresses other patterns for the moment. So the main pattern is self-defining and we proceed along it. There is no magic here: it is all explained in my book 'The Mechanism of Mind'.

If, however, we somehow enter the side track from another point, then we can travel back to the main track with ease. This is what we call the 'asymmetry of patterns'. We move along the main track only in one direction but can move back along the side track. This asymmetry is the basis both for humor and for lateral thinking. In humor the humorist takes us across to the side track and allows us to zoom our way back. In lateral thinking the various techniques of provocation help to move us across to the side track.

We can only recognize a creative idea as valuable if there is a track back from that idea to where we started. We will only accept it as valuable *if there is a logical path* to the idea. In fact we can only recognize a creative idea if it is logical in hindsight. There may be lots of other creative ideas which are but noises to us since we have no logical path of recognition.

To suppose that because a creative idea is logical in hindsight that it should also be logically available in foresight is completely to misunderstand the behavior of patterning systems. That is precisely what *we have always done*. It is a very serious matter indeed and a fundamental defect in our thinking culture.

This is why it is so important to understand the nature of patterning systems. Traditional word-based logic and philosophy is simply incapable of understanding creativity. That is why it has always seemed such a mystery.

TECHNIQUES OF LATERAL THINKING

I have written several practical books on the techniques of lateral thinking and I do not intend to go into details here. I shall, however, mention some points in order to show how deliberate techniques of creativity can be applied.

If perception is a patterning system — and it is very hard to see how it could be anything else — then something like these techniques are an essential part of thinking. They are not a luxury. They are necessary in order to escape from patterns and to cut across to new patterns.

MOVEMENT

The judgment idiom is basic to normal thinking. Does this fit experience? Is it correct? Will it work? If the idea does not fit experience it is rejected. That is normal to the argument mode, as I discussed in an earlier section.

For lateral thinking we need to exchange judgment for a different idiom. The new idiom is 'movement'. Where does this idea take me? What does this suggest? What can I get from this? What is the movement value of this idea?

Judgment is like prose: it is the 'backward' or descriptive value of what is. Movement is like poetry: it is the 'forward' or potential value of what may be.

Any idea, no matter how incorrect or illogical, can be used for its movement value. Radar was invented because someone used the movement value of the absurd idea that a radio beam could be used to shoot down airplanes.

An understanding of the idiom of movement is essential to an understanding of lateral thinking.

PROVOCATION

There may not be a reason for saying something until after it has been said.

That statement is totally contrary to normal logic and yet defines provocation. The purpose of a provocation is to get us to look at things in a different way. A scientific hypothesis is in a way a provocation. So were Einstein's thought experiments. What is interesting is that Western science made progress not because of the employment of the dialectic method in attacking or defending hypotheses — as most Western scientists believe —but because of the provocative value of an hypothesis (which Chinese science never had).

Without the movement idiom provocation would be pointless. We would simply reject the idea immediately upon the application of judgment. But movement allows us to use the provocation as a stepping stone — in order to see where we can go.

So the combination of provocation and movement is fundamental to lateral thinking.

How logical is this procedure? It is perfectly logical in a patterning universe. We use provocation to get us out of the main track. Then we use movement in order to move across to a new track. Once we are there then we may find our way back to the starting point — but with a new idea. It is the asymmetry of patterns which makes it logical to obtain new entry points into the system. We need provocation to force us out of existing patterns.

A provocation can be much more extreme than an hypothesis (which has to be reasonable). We use judgment on an hypothesis but we use movement on a provocation.

THE NEW WORD 'PO'

Many years ago I invented the new word 'po' as a language signal to indicate that the speaker was putting forward a provocation. The word 'po' signaled that a statement was being offered outside the judgment system and specifically for its provocation value.

Po, the factory should be downstream of itself.

This is an illogical impossibility with regard to the building of a factory on a river. But the provocation leads directly to the suggestion that to reduce pollution a factory should be required by legislation to place its input downstream of its own output (and so would have to be more concerned about cleaning up the water).

Po, we increase the eyes of the police instead of increasing their number.

This provocation was in connection with the problem of street crime which was amongst some problems given to me by the editor of New York

Magazine in 1971. From the provocation came the idea of making citizens the extra eyes of the police. This suggestion was published in the magazine in 1971. Since then the 'citizens' watch' concept has come to be used in 20,000 communities in the U.S.A. and has been credited with considerable reduction in certain types of crime.

Po, planes should land upside down.

This provocation seems total nonsense but 'movement' from it leads to the idea of downward lift. This in turn suggests some way of giving a negative bias to planes as they come in to land. If there was a sudden need for extra lift the negative bias could be immediately canceled — so providing an instant reservoir of lift.

There are many formal ways of setting up provocations. There are also formal ways of getting movement from an idea. There is no mystery about it. Each operation is logical in itself.

A surprisingly simple and effective technique for getting a new entry point is to use a 'random word'. On any logical basis this is absolute nonsense because by definition a random word can have nothing whatever to do with the matter in hand. Yet in a patterning system this random starting point is perfectly logical. In practice the idea works very well indeed and many creative people now use the technique automatically. This random word technique is a good illustration of why it is necessary to understand the 'system basis' of perception in order to develop thinking tools. Playing with words is just not enough.

THE ACCEPTANCE OF IDEAS

One of the difficulties of creativity is that any new idea has to be evaluated and accepted in terms of the old ideas. It is rarely possible to try out ideas directly. The suggestion of a group of children trained in lateral thinking, that a chemical plant solve the problem of getting people to work a weekend shift by employing a special and permanent weekend labor force, was not easily accepted. The suggestion ran counter to all experience of workforce motivation. In fact it was tried out and proved a great success.

So the designer of ideas has the twin task of designing ideas that will work and at the same time designing ideas that will be acceptable in terms of the old idioms by which the ideas will be judged. This is a hard task but it is the normal design task. No one can be expected to act upon an idea which does not seem to make sense. Provocation is only a stage. At the end a creative idea must be practical and make sense.

LATERAL THINKING AND CONFLICT THINKING

Lateral thinking is one of the thinking tools required for the design approach to conflict resolution. Many design schools around the world have been using my books on lateral thinking as required reading for several years now. The changing of concepts and perceptions is a key part of the design process.

Lateral thinking can be used simply to give a new direction for thinking. Thereafter logic and experience can move forward in that direction. Lateral thinking can be used to solve a particular problem. Lateral thinking can be used to provide a concept at a defined point: 'we need a concept to . . .'.

Lateral thinking is both a general style of thinking (movement and provocation) and also a set of tools that can be applied in a deliberate fashion. A senior executive of the Bank of America in the Hong Kong branch told me how he and his colleagues had used the random word technique to design a new investment instrument.

Lateral thinking is a matter of understanding, skill and experience. The provision of this is yet a further task for the third party role in triangular thinking.

SUMMARY

Concept evolution is not good enough. We need ways of backtracking out of dead-end concepts. We need ways of freeing up elements imprisoned in obsolete concepts in order to use them in better designs.

Culturally we have never been able to understand the basis of creativity because we have not understood the self-organizing nature of perception. Because any valuable creative idea must be logical in hindsight (otherwise we could never recognize the idea), we erroneously believe that such ideas could be reached in foresight through better logic. This is nonsense.

Lateral thinking is a more specific term than creativity and is concerned with pattern changing. There is movement instead of judgment. There is the setting up of provocations and the new word 'po' to signal the provocations. There are techniques which can be used deliberately to carry out defined creative tasks.

Lateral thinking is a key ingredient in design thinking and therefore a key ingredient in the designed outcome approach to conflict resolution.

CHAPTER 14

THE THIRD PARTY ROLE IN CONFLICT THINKING

The plain purpose of the third party is to convert a two-dimensional fight into a three-dimensional exploration leading to the design of an outcome.

Conflict thinking should not be a fight but a design exercise.

In this section I shall be writing about the third party role in general. Later in the book I shall introduce the S.I.T.O. concept. S.I.T.O. (Supranational Independent Thinking Organization) is specifically designed to provide a third party role in conflict thinking — and to provide a supranational focus for thinking for all occasions.

It is the essential nature of the third party role in the design approach to conflict resolution that creates the concept of 'triangular thinking'. The third party is not an addition or an aid but an integral part of the process.

I want to make it very clear that what I have in mind is not compromise nor consensus. Nor is it negotiation in the usual sense of that word. It is not arbitration nor is it bargaining. *It is quite simply design.*

It is normal in a conflict situation for both parties to start off with full confidence in the strength of their case, their muscle and their stamina. A point is then reached where it becomes obvious that neither side is likely to gain an easy victory. It now becomes a matter of hanging on: in the hope that the other side will give up or because there is no easy way out. In the end exhaustion creates the setting for a negotiated face-saving compromise. None of this has anything to do with the design of an optimal outcome. The final negotiation is a rescue patch-up rather than a constructive design.

THE NEED FOR A THIRD PARTY

From time to time throughout this book I have pointed out aspects of thinking which would have to be carried out by a third party. There are two types of reason why these things have to be carried out by a third party.

1. Because the parties involved in the conflict are bogged down by tradition, training and complacency, in the argument mode of thinking. Because the parties involved simply do not have the necessary skill or experience in lateral thinking and the design idiom.

2. Because with the best will in the world, the parties involved in the conflict simply cannot carry out certain thinking operations because these would not be consistent with their position in the conflict. The structure of the situation is such that these things simply cannot be done.

With regard to the first set of reasons there is a practical necessity for the third party. With regard to the second set of reasons there is a logical necessity for the third party.

I should also add that intention coupled with an understanding of the design needs is not an adequate substitute for expertise in the type of thinking required. Understanding sculpture does not make a person a sculptor. Thinking is not just the possession of intelligence. Thinking is the operating *skill* with which intelligence acts upon experience.

I shall now spell out the sort of functions that would be performed by the third party in the triangular thinking mode.

MOOD AND ATTITUDE

Oil and water do not mix. The addition of an emulsifying agent results in an emulsion in which very tiny drops of oil are mixed in with the water. The result is a mixture for all practical purposes. It would be the role of the third party to set the scene and the mood so that the parties involved in the conflict were able to interact in an agreeable manner. Experience has shown that the right setting can contribute considerably to the way discussions proceed. A prevailing mood of hostility limits the concepts available, as I have mentioned in an earlier section. There is no need for hostility to be signaled in an emotional sense when it has already been made apparent by the positions taken. In practice a third party can do much to change a hostile mood whereas the parties involved can do very little.

STEER AWAY FROM CONFLICT MODE

It is extremely easy for an exploratory discussion to slip back into the conflict mode. It is rather like a routine husband-and-wife quarrel. This may start about something trivial but in no time at all has slipped into a mutual exchange of hostilities about much more basic matters.

It is the role of the third party to detect these conflict initiatives and to defuse them immediately.

'The purpose of this discussion is not to show who is wrong.'

With experience, a skilled third party can make a conflict initiative seem crude and out of place.

STAGES AND AGENDA

The third party sets the stages for the exploration and design exercises. One stage is tackled at a time and there is a need for a strict stage discipline. This is important otherwise there will be an attempt to discuss everything at once in the usual argument mode.

The agenda is not set through a process of consultation with the parties involved. It is set directly by the third party. This is because an agenda can often be chosen to suit one particular line of argument rather than another. Ideally an agenda should cut across the lines of argument rather than reflect these lines. If the parties do not like the agenda that is too bad.

THINKING DIRECTIONS

The third party is the circus ringmaster or the orchestral conductor. It is the role of the third party to call for the specific thinking operations at any point. Instead of point-to-point thinking in which discussion just flows from point to point, there is structure. There are specific thinking operations to be carried through. For example the third party may call for an A.D.I. (areas of agreement, disagreement and irrelevance). The third party may also request a particular thinker to adopt a particular 'thinking hat' (for example the black hat of logical negativity).

The third party should not be tentative or pleading nor should there be a classroom atmosphere. It is more like the playing of a 'thinking keyboard'. A request is both definite and defined.

If a request is not complied with this is repeated and the failure to comply is made visible.

MAPPING AND THINK-2

The various tools for the mapping stage of thinking can be requested. There can be a demand for priorities (F.I.P.) or for alternatives (A.P.C.). There may be a request to consider the views of other people involved (O.P.V.). The third party may ask that some suggestion be extended forward in time in order to map what might happen (C. & S.). There can be a delineation of values, concerns and fears.

As I made clear in the section on mapping, each operation is carried out in isolation in its own right. There is no attempt at the time to fit the particular piece of the map into the total map. So any attempt to turn a mapped item into the basis of an argument point must be resisted.

The rules of Think-2 have to be strictly adhered to. At first this will seem artificial and will be resented. After a time the discipline will be welcomed because it relieves the thinker of having to keep the total picture in mind at every moment. A fairly short time is allocated to each operation. In time this gets people to focus directly on the operation instead of drifting back into a general discussion. It is amazing how much thinking can be done in as short a time as three minutes — provided it is focused thinking.

FOCUS

At a broad level, 'focus' is involved in defining the stages and the agenda. At a more detailed level it is the role of the third party to define a focus from time to time.

'Let's just focus on compensation.'

Setting the focus is one side of the matter; keeping people directed towards the focus is another. It is also the role of the third party to remind the thinkers of the focus of the moment.

Once the direction has been set then it becomes a matter of finding how to advance in that direction.

'In what way can we make this course of action unappealing?'

I prefer to talk in terms of setting design tasks and defining attention areas than to talk about 'asking the right questions'. This is because a question implies that an answer is known and the listener will tend to offer whatever answer is available to him or her. With a 'design task' it is assumed that there is not yet a satisfactory answer and that some thinking will need to be done. There is this important distinction between dialogue and design. Dialogue

127

seeks to bring forth what is there. Design seeks to create what is not yet anywhere.

BOGGED DOWN

When discussion has become bogged down, it is up to the third party to restart it. This can be done by shifting attention to another matter or by the third party putting in some further ideas.

When no new ideas are forthcoming it may be useful to use a deliberate stimulating technique such as the 'random word' technique from lateral thinking. This usually opens up some new lines of thought.

It is perfectly in order for the third party to acknowledge that thinking has got bogged down at that particular point. An attempt may be made to examine why this has happened.

Calling a break is another way of coping with a discussion that has got bogged down.

CREATIVITY AND LATERAL THINKING

This is a major role for the third party. This is because the third party is likely to have more expertise than the other thinkers in this area. It is also because the third party is the only one able to offer provocations and probes. Until the creative idiom has been very firmly established, any provocation coming from one of the parties to the dispute will be regarded with the utmost suspicion by the other party. Is it a signal? Does it reflect inner thoughts? Is it a sly way of putting across a position point?

Setting the focus is a skilled task. The way a problem is defined can make a huge difference to how it is solved. The way a problem is broken down into sub-problems can simplify the thinking task and also avoid stock solutions.

There is skill required to direct attention to matters which briefly enter the discussion but are perceived to be important. Unless attention is specifically focused on such matters they may never get direct attention and will have to remain the victims of assumptions.

CUT-OFF

This is really a type of 'negative' focus. It is important to cut off discussion about a matter at a particular point. For example a constructive point may have been reached. If discussion continues the effectiveness of the achievement will be diluted and even lost. A cut-off preserves that point in perception.

There are times when a finite time may be allocated to a particular thinking operation. Here the cut-off is determined by time and should be made at the preset time — even if discussion is flowing. If there is no time discipline then the thinkers get lazy and assume an open-ended situation.

There should never be any fear of cutting off a flow of ideas. They will return later. It is important that the thinkers learn to be crisp and brief. Speeches are totally out of place. So are elaborate preambles and explanations for what is to follow.

SETTING DESIGN TASKS

It is the role of the third party to set specific design tasks. The purpose of the design has to be spelled out clearly. The acceptance frame for the design (who is going to have to like it) also has to be spelled out.

In an earlier section I mentioned the importance of setting new thinking directions.

> 'Can we design a voting system to throw out polarizing candidates?'

The third party is quite free to offer provocations of any sort and then to request the other thinkers to work from those provocations.

> 'Po, the hostages benefitted from their captivity.'

The third party is in a much better position to pursue a speculative idea and to foster a tentative idea. It is not only that the third party has less at risk but also that the mind of the third party is more free to entertain ideas. The parties to the dispute would find it very difficult to pursue any suggestion which seemed to have an initial 'negative cash flow' for their own position.

OBLIQUE IDEAS

There are times when a party to a dispute has an idea which he or she would like to put forward. This cannot be done openly because the idea might give a misleading impression. The idea may also be in the nature of a probe. For whatever reason such an idea cannot be tossed on to the table.

In such cases the idea is passed to the third party (at the discussion or during a break) and then the idea is put forward directly by the third party just as if the idea had originated with the third party. This is a classic instance of the logical necessity for the third party.

IDEA HARVESTING AND NOTICING

I have often been present at creative sessions that have seemed interesting at the time. The reports of such sessions are often unaccountably dull. It is not just that an idea is more fun to listen to than to read in cold print. It is simply that people are not very good at noticing ideas. Each person is so wrapped up in the merits of his or her own idea that other ideas do not get properly noticed.

It is very much the role of the third party to notice ideas that emerge —even if they are only a glimmer of an idea which no one else has noticed. It is the role of the third party to harvest all the creative ideas that get produced in a lateral thinking session. These ideas may be taken a bit further in order to explore the benefit that might attach to them. The third party has an improving role here. There is no need to be a passive and neutral reporter provided the input is to improve the idea.

It is extremely difficult to notice something that is not in line with our thinking. That is why the third party should have a range of ideas on the matter. In this way he or she will be able to notice many more ideas than the disputants who are limited in their perceptual repertoire by the position they have to take.

OVERVIEW

The third party can take a detached overview. The third party can look at the situation in perspective. The third party can distinguish the trees but also see the wood. The third party can look down on both the situation itself and also on the thinking that is taking place with regard to the situation.

Even though the third party is not going to use judgment, he or she is in the superior position of a judge who looks down from above on what is happening in his or her court.

The third party is at all times on the same level as the disputants but also above them. The image of a triangle suggests an equality for all three angles and yet one of them is in a superior position to the others.

The overview may sometimes be converted into a running report or even a permanent report. It should be made very clear, however, that the third party is not there as a note-taker or recorder.

CONNECTIONS

From the detached and superior viewpoint, the third party is in the best position to see the whole map. As a result the third party can make connections and can show how one matter connects up with another. The third party can also show how two things which might appear different really have much in common. The third party can also show how under certain circumstances different aims can be reconciled. The third party can make bridges. The third party can drop in a connector which suddenly brings about an insight switch of perception.

Neighbors may be unaware that they actually live very close to each other because each approaches his home by a different route. Someone with a map of the area can see at once that the neighbors are close. Similarly in a conflict situation each side may get to a certain position by means of a totally different route. The final positions are, however, very close.

Very often disputants are so driven by the 'intention' of their position that they fail to notice that there is a similarity between that position and the opponent's position. Just as the domination of a preferred hypothesis makes us unable to see evidence in an innocent manner, so the domination of a conflict position makes us unable to see where we are.

CONCEPT REVIEW

A concept review lays out the established concepts, the dominating concepts, the blocking concepts, the changing concepts, the emerging concepts and the concept needs. It is a sort of functional map that is set at *concept level*. The purpose of the concept review is to create awareness of the state of the conflict. The third party with his or her overview position is in a much better position than either of the disputants to lay out the concept review. It is not an easy task because we may use concepts without ever being able to define them. It is also often possible to extract different concepts from the same operation.

A concept review should be as rich as possible and should lay out a variety of concepts. Nevertheless these will need to be organized into functional groupings (ways of monitoring, ways of exerting pressure, etc.).

Sometimes a concept review may make the parties to a conflict instantly aware of how narrow their thinking has been.

ADDITIONAL ALTERNATIVES

A prime role for the third party is to provide alternatives additional to those so far provided. The third party may use his or her own creativity in order to design further alternatives or may subcontract this thinking to a resource team (as might be the case with S.I.T.O.).

The third party in this and other instances can have a direct thinking role. It is not only the business of the third party to organize the thinking of the others and to extract the maximum from this thinking. The third party may well come to be the major input source for alternatives, suggestions, creative ideas and provocations. For this reason the third party should have some creative skill.

In addition to alternative ideas there are alternative directions. I have mentioned these before. They are much less than ideas. We could call them 'suggested direction for solution' (sds for short).

In generating alternatives it is not just a matter of putting forward more alternatives in the hope that one of them will work. It is more a matter of creating an enriched perceptual field so that the design process can be more effective. This will happen even if no one of the alternatives is directly usable.

ACCEPTANCE AND MODIFICATION OF IDEAS

The second part of the design process is the acceptance of the design by the client. The third party can take a designed outcome and then test it for acceptance with each of the involved parties separately. This is something which can only be done by a third party. An involved party could never offer a designed outcome in a neutral manner because anything offered would be seen as embodying its own wishes.

If necessary, the designed outcome can be modified by the third party in order to increase its acceptance. There were several drafts of the Camp David agreement which were offered to Begin and Sadat separately.

It is up to the third party to assess whether it is worth trying to modify the current design of outcome in order to make it acceptable, or whether it is better to abandon it and look at a new design. Certainly it should never be felt that an existing design can always be modified to give a final design. This is not so. We have seen that in patterning systems a wrong track will not evolve into something useful.

OTHER THIRD PARTY FUNCTIONS

In this section I have written mainly about the 'thinking' functions of the third party when all three parties are meeting together to design an outcome to a conflict.

There are many other third party roles that are not directly concerned with thinking. For example, a dispute may be referred to S.I.T.O. in order to take the heat out of the situation or in order to create a time gap. Similarly a party that knows that it is going to lose the conflict might prefer to lose the conflict to a S.I.T.O. opinion rather than to the other party. I shall be discussing such 'positional' third party roles when I describe the functions of S.I.T.O. in a later section.

ACCEPTANCE OF THE THIRD PARTY ROLE

Parties involved in a conflict may not always welcome the third party role. If a party feels that the exercise of force or the righteousness of its case will lead to total victory then any third party involvement is seen as likely to reduce the gains of that victory since any design would be short of total victory.

The parties in a conflict also tend to feel that the conflict is their business. This is not always the case. A brawl in a bar is the business of the bartender and the other drinkers as well as the business of the fighters. Indeed, conflicts would be less attractive if it was expected that others would automatically be involved.

There are a number of reasons why a third party role might be rejected.

It is no business of the third party.
The third party cannot know enough about the scene.
The third party does not have the feel and idiom for the situation.
The third party can be irresponsible.
The third party has nothing at stake and does not have to live with the result.
The third party is just playing around.
The third party is an academic theorist with no knowledge of the real world.
For one reason or another the third party is seen as favoring the other side.
The third party is unlikely to produce anything different from what would emerge anyway.

There may be a time for the third party — but not yet and not until all hope of complete victory is gone.

The third party should only be a go-between negotiator who does not seek to contribute any ideas as such.

Neither party will reveal the confidential information on which their positions are really based (military) and hence a design exercise is futile.

All these objections are based on a satisfaction with the argument mode of thinking and the view that a third party will only interfere with this. Once the inadequacy of the argument mode is understood and publicized then it will be seen as negligent and aggressive to wish to conduct a conflict in that manner.

ENTREPRENEURIAL STYLE

The third party should be effective and entrepreneurial and should show skill and flair. The third party role is not just a neutral administrative function that could be handled by a bureaucracy. There is a need for the flair of a good lawyer, although the style of thinking is quite different. Perhaps it should be the flair of an architect, which combines creativity with practicality in a design that has to be generally accepted.

PART IV CONFLICT

CHAPTER 15

CONFLICT MODELS

E very designer has in his or her mind a repertoire of standard designs. The designer would hardly expect to get paid for a job if he or she simply recommended a standard design, but even when the design is 'totally' new many of the idioms will have been inspired by features in existing designs. In this section I shall be looking at some models of conflict. This is not an exhaustive list. The choice has been made because each model illustrates some different aspect of conflict.

ATHLETICS RACE

The emphasis is on formalized conditions which are set up precisely to help the competition of ability. The athletes compete against each other only indirectly. Each exerts his or her maximum effort. There is no attempt to interfere with the effort of others (by and large). At every moment there is a consciousness of how things are going. The prize is mainly symbolic. There are a whole range of concepts, of which perhaps the most important is parallel exertion and non-interference. The formality of the setting and disqualification for breaking the rules are essential background concepts.

SOCCER

Formality of setting and fixed method of achievement. The scoring of goals is a crucial concept in terms of 'score-keeping'. In many conflict situations score-keeping of one sort or another is the only way either side can claim victory. What would a soccer match be like if the goal posts were removed? What would terrorism be like if there were no media mention of successes? There are numerous rules in soccer. These are designed to prevent one side from gaining an unfair advantage. Unlike in athletics, breaking a rule does not lead to instant disqualification but to an immediate penalty. The decision of the umpire is instant and final. The key concepts are score-keeping and the instant small punishments for wrongdoing.

BUSINESS COMPETITION

An open market in which different manufacturers compete. They compete on price, quality, advertising and distribution. The more successful become even more successful. The less successful have to change or they go under. There is some brand loyalty but nothing like that in politics. A consumer will switch purchases according to what is being offered. The motivation is appeal. Fear is totally absent on the part of the consumer. From time to time manufacturers seek to protect their markets by blocking imports. Efficiency, effectiveness and product design are key factors in the competition. Multiple small decisions, and repeat decisions, determine the outcome of the competition. It is assumed that the consumer knows what he or she wants and can assess the value of the product. The key concept is that the competition or conflict is ultimately decided by the consumer in terms of consumer benefits. Nevertheless the competition is also decided by the effectiveness of the organization in getting something worthwhile to the consumer.

AUCTION SALE

A direct competition on cost. Each side determines how valuable the item is and pays the appropriate cost. That cost is solely determined by the cost estimation of the other side. How long do you go on bidding? At what cost does it stop being worthwhile? A key factor is that at any point a bidder can simply drop out. When a bidder drops out he incurs no cost at all. We could look at industrial strike action as a form of auction. Each side is prepared to pay the rising price of pain and discomfort (loss of wages, loss of production). The point is reached where one side reaches its bidding limit: it is not worth going on. The trouble is that the losing bidder still pays a heavy cost. It is more like a flagellation competition. The key concept of the auction model is the *offering* of prices so that each party determines the value of the object for himself or herself.

MARKET BARGAINING

You might argue that market bargaining is but a form of auction with each party starting at opposite ends of the price scale. There are important differences. Market bargaining is more a trading of values. You might buy two instead of one. This other object will be thrown in as well. There is a value to the stall-holder of your buying at this moment rather than later. The stall-holder talks up the value of what is offered. Each side seeks to explore and exploit the values of the other side. Because of the concept of variable value (where something is of more value to one party than to another) it is possible to give value without losing value. This is the idealized model of collective bargaining. But if the prospective purchaser picked up the ceramic vase and held it out in front of him, threatening to drop it if he did not get his price, that would be something different.

CUTTING THE CAKE

This is an extremely effective conflict resolution model from the nursery. Two children are squabbling over the division of a cake between them. The traditional solution is simple: 'You cut and I choose'. This way the person making the division strives to be as fair as possible because any obvious unfairness will only be to his or her disadvantage. The nearest we get to it in adult conflict resolution is for one party to set out alternative proposals and for the other party to choose one of these. This is not really equivalent for all the proposals may be heavily in favor of the party putting them forward. In the cake idiom the key concept is the separation of design and choice in such a way that an unfair design penalizes the designer.

ARM WRESTLING

Consider a macho bar-room scene. Two hefty types are squaring up for a fight to show who is the dominant male in the area. The fight takes place. There are broken chairs, tables, bottles and even noses. It is a messy business. It would need to happen with every challenge to the temporarily dominant male. Contrast all this with the simplicity and elegance of arm wrestling. The two contenders sit down at a table and lock arms. In a few minutes it is all over. There is a clear victor and clear loser. It is so quietly done that even the beer glass on the table has not spilled a drop. This condensation of a messy conflict into a brief and decisive trial of strength is remarkable. It is, of course, a key factor that the person who seems likely to win at arm wrestling looks as if he might also have won at a full-scale fight. This is important because it is a genuine 'sample' of strength that is being tested. It is not like

139

setting out to determine male supremacy by a card game or a darts match. The key concept is then the testing of a relevant sample of strength instead of having to deploy full strength.

THE LAW COURTS

The traditional method for conflict resolution. A formal setting is provided and there is a competition between the lawyers on the opposing sides. Unlike the athletics race, however, the outcome is not self-evident but is decided by judge or jury. The decision is made by referring the presented facts and claims to an existing 'code' of law. Society also has the means to enforce the judgment of the court. The key concepts are therefore: a reference code; a way of referring conflict to this code; a means of enforcing the conclusion.

ARBITRATION

A procedure in which both parties decide upon an outside assessment of the merits of their respective cases. In essence the conflict is turned over to a third party. The parties have made the assessment that the cost of prolonging the conflict is likely to be much greater than any loss due to imperfection of the arbitration. Both sides have also decided that full victory is no longer a possibility. The key concept is the trade-off between the value of prolonging the conflict and getting it solved, even if imperfectly.

GREENMAIL

This is a Wall Street term relating to a type of alleged blackmail. A corporation buys up the stock of another corporation in order to launch a takeover bid. For various reasons the takeover bid fails. The bought-up stock is still held by the bidder and with that stock goes the possibility of creating trouble for the company. So the management of the company decide to buy out the bidder for a high figure. This means that someone can make a great deal of money by just threatening to take over another corporation and then getting bought out. The key principle is that the aggressor does not go away empty handed. In a sense the aggressor is bought off. This is always a very difficult point in conflict resolution. Should the aggressor be rewarded in any way, should the aggressor be sent away empty handed or should the aggressor be severely punished for the aggression? The traditional view is that to reward an aggressor in any way simply encourages aggression. An aggressor will 'try it on' knowing that at the end of the day there will be some reward even if not the full one (as is the case with greenmail on Wall Street). The alternative view is that an aggressor who is in a strong position is hardly likely to just pack up and go home with nothing. This means that the aggressor has to be defeated and that can be costly. The natural bias is so much against the appeasement of blackmail that the matter is not always fully investigated. Clearly there should be a distinction made between deliberate aggression (as with Hitler's expansion in Europe) and conflicts that arise (as with the Falklands).

PRESSURE GROUPS

The characteristic of a pressure group is that it does not expect to succeed immediately. It is a matter of creating an awareness, a visibility and a public consciousness. Like a manufacturer selling a product, the pressure group works through the decisions of others: media, voters and politicians. The purpose of the group is to maintain public consciousness on an issue (and initially to focus it upon that issue). This is usually done by creating events which the media cannot resist. As soon as something has become a public issue then every politician has to assess whether it is going to be to his benefit to ignore it, back it or oppose it. So such groups work through the existing system of media and democracy. It should also be said that, quite apart from political action, the attention generated by protest groups can work over a long term to achieve considerable changes in attitude towards different things (environment, women's rights, product safety, etc.). These do end up by being cultural changes. The key concept is the 'steady pressure'.

SYSTEM BREAKDOWN

It may be argued that many of the conflict idioms mentioned here only operate within a given system (like the courts of law or a soccer field) and that much conflict arises precisely from a *breakdown* of systems.

There are two answers to this objection. The first is that we need to design more and better systems so that when breakdown occurs in one system there is another system that can still operate. For instance, when two parties to a conflict break off direct communication they should still be able to communicate with each other through a structure such as S.I.T.O. or the Red Cross.

The second answer is that even though a particular system has broken down the parties may still be operating in a wider system. For instance, locally fighting nations may still belong to the United Nations or the Commonwealth or treaty alliances. In the end there is the automatic system which includes both conflicting parties. That is not a formal system but it is nevertheless a system with its own logic and dynamics.

CONFLICT AND COMPETITION

Many of the models put forward in this section will seem to have been models of competition rather than conflict. In fact all conflict can be seen as competition. There is a desire for a particular end and the other party has a desire for a different end. Conflict is only *one way* of carrying out this competition. It is rather like an athlete spiking an opponent in order to win a race. The conflict mode of competing is simple and powerful. If you conquer your enemy then you can achieve whatever you wish (women, land or goods). Because of this all-embracing competition mode called conflict, it often happens that the real purpose of the competition is forgotten. Conflict which was really just a means to an end becomes an end in itself. Indeed the pursuit of the conflict for its own sake may actually destroy what was desired in the first place. If in order to take over some oil wells you have to destroy the oil wells then the exercise is pointless.

It is always worth remembering that conflict is never an end in itself. It is either a way of competing for something or a way of escaping from a clash of interests.

So in any design exercise (which is what this book is about) it is always worth asking whether the underlying competition needs can be achieved in a way other than conflict.

CHAPTER 16

CONFLICT FACTORS

A designer works with his materials and with the idioms of his field. A boat designer works with fiberglass, wood and metal and with the idioms of naval architecture. A graphic designer works with colors, paper, printing processes and with the idioms of communication. In considering the application of the design process to conflict resolution we need to take a look at some of the fundamental idioms involved.

A treatise on the origins, causes and evolution of concepts would be lengthy indeed. It would also focus on the analytical approach: let us understand the causes and try to remove them. The design idiom is more forward looking. What are the ingredients that we have to put together to design a solution? Listing all these ingredients would also be a lengthy task and does not fit in with the purpose of this book. My purpose here is to take a look at some of the conflict factors that would be relevant to a designer.

I have simplified the factors into four groupings, all of which happen to start with the letter 'F'.

Fear
Force
Fair
Funds

There is a good deal of overlap between these factors but they serve as useful organizing points. In the following sections I shall treat each of these in turn.

CHAPTER 17

CONFLICT FACTORS:
FEAR

Fear is always about the future. It is always about something that may happen. There may be fear of condemnation, fear of retaliatory force or fear of the high cost of a conflict. So there is bound to be an overlap between fear and force and also the other factors.

From a design point of view fear is a powerful and subtle ingredient since it can operate permanently. The fear of being electrocuted operates so long as the electric wire is present. Fear can also have a high amplifying value. If one old lady a month is mugged in a certain town then every single old lady in that town may be afraid to go out at night even though the odds of getting mugged are quite low. In Northern Ireland, in almost every year of the troubles, the deaths from road accidents have exceeded the deaths from violence.

In the control of crime, fear of being punished — even severely — is not enough if every criminal believes that he, personally, will not get caught. To the fear of punishment must be added the fear of getting caught. That is why an informer system tends to be effective: it greatly increases the fear of being caught.

As an ingredient fear has some great weaknesses. The first is that it may not work at all for someone who is stupid or who has insufficient imagination to see what might happen. It also does not work for the foolhardy or brave or those who derive an adrenalin kick from living dangerously.

Another weakness is that one fear can drive out another. The terrified young man may enlist in the army through fear of being considered a coward or fear of being prosecuted as a draft dodger. He goes into battle through fear of letting his mates down, fear of the sergeant or fear of the concept of disobedience. In the Falklands War President Galtieri was frightened that if he pulled out of the Islands Argentina would be humiliated and his government and his life would be forfeit. His best bet was to stay put and to hope for some sort of victory.

A negotiator for the P.L.O. was murdered by hardliners simply because he had been willing to negotiate. Fear often prevents negotiations because the negotiator would fear punishment or at least losing the support of his followers.

There is fear of defeat and fear of humiliation. There is the great fear of being seen to be a loser. It could be argued that the reason the British war fleet was sent to the Falklands was really the fear of humiliation. The preservation of a self-image on a personal or national level is extremely important and fear of losing that image is a strong motivator. Indeed, Enoch Powell goaded Mrs Thatcher in the House of Commons with exactly this approach: how could she, of all people, stand for this Argentine insult. The stronger a self-image the more vulnerable it is to manipulation in this manner.

THIN END OF THE WEDGE

I have mentioned elsewhere in this book how a trivial incident can give rise to a serious conflict through this 'thin end of the wedge' idiom. The notion is that it only takes the insertion of the thin end of the wedge into a great rock for the rock eventually to be cracked clean into half. So a trivial incident must be resisted because of the anticipation of all the things it could lead to. Of course there is some justification in this idiom. After all, the early appeasement of Hitler led to just such a creep strategy. Unfortunately the idiom can be applied to *anything at all*. Because fear is only limited by the imagination of the person doing the fearing, any incident at all can be seen as leading to great disasters. Thereafter it is up to the persuasive power of that person to convince others that mighty things are at stake. This idiom also has to do with the image idiom. In the gunboat days, when wars were fought over the molesting of a British national in foreign parts, there was a mixture of image preservation and also the inconvenience to trade if this sort of thing became a habit.

RETALIATION

There is massive retaliation where a small incident invites severe reprisals. This is often not credible because launching the massive reprisal requires a major decision which rarely seems justified at the time by the small incident. As the first and the second incident pass then fear of the reprisal must fade. Indeed, it would now be too late to launch a reprisal since it could only have punishment value and no deterrent value any more (because it would no longer be seriously expected). For this reason the measured response reprisal as used by Israel is becoming more relevant. A terrorist raid would be followed by a jet attack on a P.L.O. camp.

This tit-for-tat retaliation may become a feature of modern conflicts. When the British Government expelled the Nigerian High Commissioner for alleged knowledge of the attempt to kidnap a Nigerian in exile in London, the Nigerian Government responded with a measured tit-for-tat. The holding of the hostages in the American Embassy in Teheran was a sort of tit-for-tat for the U.S. giving shelter to the Shah.

The Russian boycott of the Los Angeles Olympics was an exact retaliation for the U.S. boycott of the Moscow Olympics.

The disadvantage of the tit-for-tat idiom is that it completely ignores the justification for the first action because in the eyes of the victim that first act was not justified. Tit-for-tat is also open to any nation, no matter how small. In a sense it creates an immense number of hostages around the world.

The advantage of the tit-for-tat idiom is that it is finite and measured. It is an act which is complete in itself. It need not escalate into a more serious conflict. Another advantage is that it may help to prevent wrongdoing by making visible a practical response.

DETERRENCE

This is a huge area and covers everything from mutual nuclear deterrence to fear of condemnation by the General Council of the United Nations. In a way nuclear deterrence only works because of some doubts about the sanity of the other side. Suppose Russia were suddenly to sweep into Austria. After the allotted time of conventional N.A.T.O. defense there would need to be a decision to go nuclear. Would the world really want to launch a full-scale war just to rescue Austria? The sensible answer might be 'no'. But because the Russians cannot quite rely on that sensible answer they might be deterred. On the other hand, if the Russians were genuinely concerned about the possibility of a nuclear first strike from a European-based missile then this fear could easily be overcome by placing first strike decision of nuclear weapons in the hands of the host nation. Would it be conceivable that the Netherlands or Italy would choose to launch a first strike nuclear attack on the U.S.S.R?

For deterrence to work there has always got to be a balance between the gain and the loss. Where there is not very much to be gained then deterrence will work very well. Why take a big risk for a very small gain? This is why Kruschev withdrew the missiles from Cuba. That is why nuclear deterrence may work in Europe. If a modest jewel is surrounded by an electrified fence then that jewel may be safe. If a very valuable jewel is protected in the same way the protection may not work.

It follows, then, that if the gains of victory are slight then deterrence works well. So perhaps we should direct some thinking towards methods of making an occupation of another country difficult and valueless. For example we might design anti-personnel weapons so cheaply that millions could be buried in a country. Each little rod would emit gamma radiation so a passerby could give a tiny dose of radiation to any unwelcome visitor. If this happened hundreds of times then that visitor would die. This would be a sort of democratic violence since it required an accumulation of 'death-votes'. This suggestion is only a metaphor for a way of making occupation difficult. The Swiss use the same idiom with their intense military training so that any invasion of Switzerland would be costly in proportion to any benefits gained.

FEAR OF DEFEAT

Fear of defeat can stop parties embarking on a conflict in the first place. Once the conflict is under way then — paradoxically — the fear of defeat tends to keep the conflict going. This is because any way out will usually be constructed as a 'defeat' for one side or the other. That party would rather delay that moment of defeat and also wants to hang on in the hope that something might turn up. Our ability to design 'ways out' which are not 'defeats' is crucial in this regard. We find this difficult to do since each side in the conflict knows the other side to be wrong and wrongdoing must be punished by defeat. To design a rewarding way out for a party to a conflict goes clean against our basic idiom of a conflict as a fight to the end. As I have said elsewhere in this book, we need to put a lot of design effort in exactly at this point. A way out is a way out and not a defeat.

CHAPTER 18

CONFLICT FACTORS: FORCE

If there was no force could there be any conflict? There are clashes of interest and conflicts even within nunneries where there is no apparent use of force. There are all sorts of force, quite apart from physical force. In the nunnery there might be moral force, emotional force, withdrawal of co-operation, withdrawal of approval and all sorts of subtle uses of force. Non-co-operation, as in Gandhi's India or the withdrawal of labor in a strike, is an obvious example of persuasive force. There is system pain as well as physical pain. When a system breaks down then those who were benefiting from the system get discomforted and pained.

Force is used to start conflicts, to energize them and to end them. Military force and physical violence has always been the main line of argument over the ages. Power comes from the barrel of a gun, as Mao used to say. Arguments that have strong physical support have tended to win through —at least for the time being.

In personal physical combat some cultures have developed highly skilled methods of combating superior force by means of skill. Such methods as judo or aikido tend to use the force of the assailant to defeat the assailant. In terms of group force we have never designed anything remotely comparable. The nearest we might get is by means of bodies like the United Nations where the complaints of a small bullied nation might bring down the censure of all other nations on the aggressor.

It is certainly true that technology is changing the whole idiom of military force. Missiles are matched against missiles and all the bravery in the world will not alter the technical balance. Muscle power becomes less significant. A superior missile system will outperform an inferior one by a great margin. Aircraft with superior missiles will shoot down aircraft with inferior missiles by a factor of several to one. An infantryman with a small shoulder-launched missile can knock out a large tank. This means that massive armies do not have the advantage they always had. It also means that a small group of men can be trained to use sophisticated weapons that have been imported from another country. It almost leads one to suppose that the day will come when a technical matching of weapon performances will substitute for physical warfare. The weapon systems will be compared and it will be decided which country has the advantage for the moment.

Trying them out in real life will be wasteful, costly and pointless. If such elements as surprise can be designed out of the system then there is little point in real combat except to test the organizational capabilities of each side. If a missile automatically triggers an anti-missile missile then the exercise is futile — hence the 'Star Wars' approach of President Reagan.

To some extent limited wars have become weapon testing systems (Israel-Syria, Iraq-Iran, etc.) Surrogate wars have become ideological testing systems.

BIG POWER

Big bombs and the ability to deliver them symbolize big power. Economic resources and technical skill produce the weaponry. Smaller countries cannot produce these things but they can buy them. If there were no arms trade then local wars would be rather difficult. In the end Argentina was not able to match the British missile for missile even though the French-made Exocet missiles used by Argentina were technically very good. Big power is ultimately in the control of big power countries and it is the willingness of these countries to sell or make available these systems that controls local conflicts. A certain amount of control is already exerted by the big powers, who do not supply smaller nations with the more powerful missile systems. There is no limit on the supply of conventional war toys on the basis that these would simply be supplied from elsewhere (and the sales revenue lost).

INTERRUPTIVE POWER

It is rather easier to put a block of concrete on to a railway line and so derail a train than it is to design a locomotive and build a railroad. The power to interrupt and destroy will always be greater than the power to prevent it happening. So guerilla and terrorist movements have an advantage in terms of action. The key point is whether this action can achieve anything. A guerilla movement that advances to become a civil war might then achieve what an ordinary war might achieve: takeover of a country. Below that potential a guerilla movement can only serve to keep attention on an issue, to destabilize a government, or as a sense of mission for its members. It must be

149

extremely rare for any guerilla movement ever to get itself into a negotiating position because the members would become individually vulnerable once they became visible. Theoretically a guerilla group could bargain with a government for certain rights and then 'go quiet' if these were granted. The movement would then be reactivated if required. The trouble is that the group would lose its momentum in the quiet period. In essence such a group would become a pressure group.

WITHHOLDING POWER

Wherever a system is operating then any member of that system has the power to halt the system by withholding co-operation. I mentioned this type of power at the beginning of this section. At the Security Conference in Madrid, Malta held up the conclusion for eight weeks by refusing to agree to the conclusions until provision was made for a Mediterranean security conference. The rules of the meeting required complete agreement so the conclusion could not be finalized. The United States withdrew from U.N.E.S.C.O. removing a quarter of the budget. The Russians walked out of the Geneva missile disarmament talks. Negotiators refuse to meet or walk out of a meeting.

In a way there is an absurdity to this type of force because it is so unconstructive and so easy to use. It can become a form of blackmail, as in the case of the quarrel between Britain and the E.E.C. over the budget. Mrs Thatcher refused to ratify new fund-raising proposals for the E.E.C. and as a result the E.E.C. refused to implement the agreed rebate on the contribution of Great Britain.

Economic sanctions are another example of withholding power.

Although this type of force is an absurdity in some ways, it is at the same time very valuable. It is valuable because it emphasizes the interlocking nature of world affairs. Because of this interlocking nature it may eventually become possible to resolve conflicts without war. The system must, however, be used with immense sensitivity. If this form of power is used on every occasion (as in the E.E.C. squabble), it becomes pointless and threatens the whole system. If each time it is used it is turned up to maximum power then it also becomes pointless since any disagreement will be at full throttle (like the Carter response to the Russian invasion of Afghanistan). There needs to be a much more sensitive control, perhaps like a fine-tuning of interest rates. If some independent body decided that your country was in the wrong then the interest rates on all international loans to your country would rise by a few base points.

This is an area which requires a great deal of careful thinking. Sanctions have usually failed either because something is needed from that country (like strategic minerals from Rhodesia or South Africa) or because individual countries have seen an economic advantage in finding a way around the sanctions. There has always been insufficient policing of these things and insufficient sanctions against the sanction busters. Traditional court systems are too slow and involved.

HOSTAGE POWER

In its crudest form this refers to the taking of hostages or to kidnapping. In system terms it is a localization of power in a focused manner when that power would be quite ineffective otherwise. What is really being held hostage is the attitude of the party attacked. It can be a family's love for its kidnapped child. It can be a country's concern for its innocent citizens.

In a similar way a nation's self-image and ideals can be held hostage inasmuch as its behavior must conform to these. So the behavior of the U.S. Government is restricted by notions of what can be done. Support for a dictatorship is difficult, especially if there is evidence of abuse of human rights or the operation of death squads. So an opponent has the power to limit the behavior of a party to what is consistent with the image of that party. In a sense that party is 'hostage' to its own image.

OPPORTUNITIES AND REWARDS

It is interesting that we always think in terms of force and restriction when it comes to conflicts. The idiom of the fight is very firmly established. It is extremely rare to think in terms of rewards, opportunities, benefits and attractions. Yet these are very powerful ways of getting human behavior to move in a certain direction. When applied to conflict, however, they are immediately classified under the concept of 'bribery'. The emotional loading of that term at once rules out any such considerations. This is a classic example of how language affects thinking. Any opportunity design at all could attract the accusation of being a bribe. In a parallel manner any party which accepted an 'opportunity' way out of a conflict would be accused of *selling out*. People expect a fight and want a fight and any other design is a disappointment. Only a very late compromise negotiation is at all acceptable.

I once suggested that it would make economic sense to give certain prisoners a pension on leaving prison. This meant that they had a means of living and would not have to go back to crime. It also meant that they now had something to lose if they reverted to crime. Since 80% of people in prison have been there before and since it costs a great deal to keep someone in prison the idea makes some sense. But it runs exactly counter to our concepts of punishment. To reward someone for being a criminal is an absurd contradiction. Similarly to reward — in any way — a party to a conflict is a moral contradiction.

MORAL FORCE

This is one of the most practical and powerful types of force in conflict situations. It ranges from the condemnation of a U.N. resolution to the persuasive pressure of friends. It is most suitably described in the section on 'fairness'. In that next section I shall be looking at the concept of wrongdoing and the breaking of codes.

CHAPTER 19

CONFLICT FACTORS:
FAIR

'It's not fair.'

From an early age children have a well-developed sense of what is not fair. If Johnny gets two biscuits and Patrick only gets one, then Patrick knows it is not fair. Children also learn that 'fairness' is a useful way to call for adult help. For some reasons adults turn out to be guardians of fairness. The moral sense of adults is readily on tap to a child.

The sense of what is fair (and just, and right) is central to civilization. We tend to think that moral restraints are rather feeble and that human nature is not much restrained by a moral sense. I am not sure that this is right. There are numerous examples of where individuals or nations have not shown the slightest moral restraint. But we should not forget that for *most of the time* people and nations do behave in a moral manner. Powerful nations could easily behave in a much more rapacious way. There is nothing to stop them except a moral sense and fear of the moral outrage of the rest of the world if they misbehave.

Where people or nations do behave contrary to morals it is often because they are following the dictates of their own set of morals which claim a higher value. The excesses of the Hitler regime were largely due to the notion of a super-race with the moral license this provided. A different view of human rights in some totalitarian regimes is due to a regard for the 'higher' moral of the welfare of the state rather than the welfare of an individual. The Catholic Inquisition carried out some pretty barbaric acts —but these were done for the moral good of society, the Church and the heretic himself. The Khomeini regime in Iran is no doubt following the higher morals of Islamic fundamentalism.

The reason I make this point is that I do believe that people are really rather moral creatures on the whole and conflict arises not from a lack of morality but from a different set of morals or from seeing things in a different way.

THE RIGHTNESS OF THE CASE

Each party in a conflict starts out by believing — or comes to believe — in the rightness of its case. The Argentinians believe that the Malvinas were properly part of Argentina since they had belonged to Spanish Argentina and on liberation should have stayed with independent Argentina. Instead a series of takeovers left them in the hands of the British. To go back to the beginning of the nineteenth century in order to establish an historical claim is really rather weak, as it would alter much of the world's map and return large parts of the U.S.A. (much of Texas) to the Mexicans. Theoretically any conquest could be challenged on the basis that it was a conquest. Curiously, the much better claim — that geographically and practically the islands are part of Argentina and are only British as a colonial relic — is not usable because geographic tidiness has never been accepted by nations as a legitimate right to sovereignty. Any Southern Ireland claim to the North is based on history and on geographical tidiness.

At other times it is much more appropriate to argue from the ethnic base of the population. You choose your source of rightness according to the case you need to make.

As I mentioned in an earlier section, there is a wide selection of multi-purpose 'justice' noises that can be put together to provide a legitimate case for many situations. Such noises include 'rights', 'parity', 'oppression', 'exploitation', 'democratic', 'freedom', 'dictatorship', 'bullying' and so on. This does not mean that these are false banners and that there is no justice in the case paraded under these banners. It simply means that it is relatively simple to put any case as a demand for justice.

THE LAW

Civilization has put together codes of law in order to simplify the task of moral judgment. Instead of having to judge each case on its moral merits, the case is referred to the law (which may be coded or built up as case law). At the same time it makes life easier for individuals since they know where they stand. Even if the law is not very explicit or comprehensive it serves a useful purpose because it provides a reference point for judge and jury in their assessment. It is said that in Hong Kong crime itself, and corruption in the police force, could be reduced to a fraction of what they are now — if only gambling ceased to be a crime. In this sense the law can create crime. Where a law is contrary to a consensus of behavior then it tends to lose its moral base. To some extent this is what happens when taxation seems excessive.

CONVENTIONS

The Geneva Convention is a remarkably successful device. The treatment of prisoners in war and the general conduct of war (from a humanitarian point of view) would not easily fit under normal law. To judge and condemn each case on its merits would lead to endless argument and justifications. The arbitrary establishment of a neutral code immediately formalizes the situation. What is permitted and what is not permitted is spelled out in sufficient detail. Anyone breaking the code knows that the code is being broken. This becomes a matter of personal guilt, of international condemnation and of loss of face for the guilty party.

We probably need a lot more codes of this type — perhaps a code for terrorist behavior.

In any country the constitution is really a convention of this sort rather than a body of law. The advantage of a convention is that it can lay down rules for behavior whereas a law only indicates what cannot be done.

Acceptable standards of human behavior and human rights are felt to be so universally accepted that any breach of them merits attack. This is what gives one country the right to interfere in what would otherwise be the internal affairs of another country.

INTERNATIONAL FORUMS

Organizations like the United Nations are set up to provide a forum in which nations can visibly pass judgment on another nation. This has two effects. The first is the visible label of wrongdoing as carried by a U.N. Resolution and made available to the public. The second effect is the 'trial' by peer pressure.

The jury idiom of peer pressure only works when the peers are neutral and independent (as in a court of law). If, however, the peers are formed into alliances and power blocs then the whole jury idiom is lost and is simply replaced by the parliamentary idiom which says that whatever your side does is right and whatever the other side does is wrong. Although the U.N. was set up as a peer group of independent nations it is now obvious that it tends to behave as alliance groupings. This means that only very severe wrongdoing can be censured and even so an 'abstention' from one's friends is the most severe penalty available.

Nevertheless the condemnation of an international body does have considerable moral value. In practical terms it may be ignored but it cannot be removed. It may be argued against but it cannot be canceled by an argument. The Israelis developed the habit of carrying out all their activity before a U.N. resolution could be organized and then stopping after it.

PEER PRESSURE

For teenagers this is the most effective form of pressure. A teenager smokes or takes drugs if his peer group do so. A teenager beats up old ladies if that is the idiom of the group. For nations and their leaders peer pressure is also very powerful. It is even more powerful when it is exerted by friends in an informal and steady manner. No one likes to be isolated. Everyone must tend to doubt their own judgment if all the people around have come to a different opinion.

Sometimes friends tend to feel that out of loyalty they should support each other even when they disagree. If you expect loyalty then you must provide it in turn. This means that friends are less likely to disagree with each other in a public forum. Therefore an informal way of bringing peer pressure to bear could be most valuable. That is one of the possible roles for S.I.T.O.

It sometimes happens that the public announcement of outrage condemns the action of an ally (as Mrs Thatcher condemned the Reagan invasion of Grenada) whilst the private message may be one of support. This is another example of the two-level type of communication I mentioned earlier in the book.

PUBLIC OPINION

Where there is a free and active media, public opinion is a powerful determinant of moral outrage. It is difficult to assess the effect of public opinion in countries with a centrally controlled press and media. Is word-of-mouth communication effective? Is there a sufficient window on other information sources?

Public opinion in other countries does seem to be a powerful influence even though it cannot change anything directly. It may just be that nations like to be liked. It may be that an ideology needs reassurance from others. It is characteristic of ideologies that they have to persuade others of the message in order to remain convinced of it.

Public opinion pressure would be more credible if it was more modulated. If any action results in screaming headlines and full throttle condemnation then it soon becomes a cliché. Instead of having the value of moral condemnation it is reduced to the triviality of party slogan: anything that side does is bad.

CHAPTER 20

CONFLICT FACTORS: FUNDS

For 'funds' read 'costs'. 'Funds' happens to start with an 'F' and so completes the four factors: fear, force, fair and funds.

The Falklands War probably cost about £2 billion. The cost of keeping a significant force on the Islands is set at about £600 million a year. There were 1,800 people on the Islands at the time. The cost of the war plus one year's support costs works out at almost £1.5 million per inhabitant. That sort of compensation might have persuaded the majority to set up home elsewhere. Of course that sort of thinking can never be employed for two reasons. The first is that moral principles are never for sale and cannot be calculated in money terms. The second is that hindsight costs cannot be calculated in foresight and — even if they were — no parliament would be willing to vote for non-military purposes the huge sums it would happily vote for military purposes.

The 1984 miners' strike in Great Britain is estimated to have cost about £70 million a week (£10 million a day). This covers loss of production, extra costs for electricity generation, extra costs in steel production, loss of taxes, etc. There comes a time when the costs must exceed the amount that was demanded to keep open uneconomic pits (the cause of the strike). Yet principles are not for sale and what is at stake is the profitability of the whole of British industry. It is claimed that giving way to the miners would enshrine the principle of uneconomic job subsidies and a final loss of world competitiveness.

The cost of most conflicts very quickly escalates beyond the point at which the conflict makes sense to either side. Cost should be the *major determinant* of the feasibility of a conflict. In practice it rarely comes in at all because of this notion that money and rights are two separate universes. In some situations such as wage bargaining it is felt that the notching upwards of the wage scale has a long-term benefit even if the local logic (what is gained against what is lost) is unfavorable.

Perhaps there should be an 'office of conflict cost estimation' in order to prepare a cost document that could be shown to both parties. Perhaps a 'conflict audit' could be prepared after the conflict in order to reveal the actual costs incurred. A certain culture of cost consciousness might tend to reduce the attractiveness of conflicts as a means of solving disputes.

If the cumulative cost of a conflict was clearly visible all along there might come a point when the parties wished to end the conflict by means of a designed outcome. Unfortunately there may be a paradox here. If the cost has escalated then the party might have to hang on to the end — for victory or defeat — because the cost has now become too high for any negotiated settlement. This was the dilemma President Galtieri found himself in. There is therefore all the more reason for designing rewards into designed outcomes even if there is no moral justification for this.

Apart from the actual cost of weaponry and loss of trade there is often an inflation cost. The war economics very often give rise to inflation (in Israel, in the U.S. after Vietnam).

Needless to say cost is not only counted in terms of money. It includes human lives and suffering, diversion of skilled manpower, agricultural neglect, cost in morale and in world image, etc.

It is quite obvious that if you have to defend your life (or your freedom), that cost does not matter. This is, however, only one aspect of conflict and it would be absurd to suppose that in all conflicts both parties were defending themselves in this manner. In all other cases cost should matter much more than it does. Unfortunately it is difficult to be convinced that if the money were not spent on the conflict it would have been spent in a visibly beneficial way elsewhere. Perhaps each country should have a conspicuous 'conflict fund' which would be used in obviously beneficial ways at the end of the year if there had been no conflict calls on that fund.

If the day came when people and nations came to realize that no one could afford conflicts, then what we now solve in this crude way would be handled in a more sophisticated manner.

CHAPTER 21

CONFLICT ATTITUDES

The unfortunate thing is that those involved in a conflict dare not admit their true conflict attitudes even to themselves. They would lose confidence and resolve and the ability to sustain their supporters if they had to admit that victory was unlikely. It has always astonished me that Frederick the Great used to lose ground and men to his enemies and still came out as the victor of the battle. It was all a matter of morale. Frederick the Great used to be convinced that he had won. His troops and soon his enemies believed that as well — even though the score card went the other way. So it is quite reasonable for both sides in a conflict to maintain attitudes of completely unrealistic confidence. At a roulette table anything can happen at the next spin of the wheel. The fact that anything can happen does not mean it is likely to happen. But when the only alternative to hope is defeat then you stay with hope. All the more reason for being able to design outcomes which would not be regarded as 'defeats'.

THE MAKING OF A CONFLICT

It has to be supposed that in most cases conflicts arise because both sides want a conflict to arise. For the moment we can exclude bullying aggression. As with the First World War, there is a feeling that there should be a conflict. The excuse for it or the immediate reasons for it are less important.

As in the animal kingdom, the purpose of this sort of conflict is to establish a 'general dominance' over the other party. The young lion must challenge the old lion. The sea-lion must show who is master to the other sea-lion that threatens the beach harem. In a pack of wolves or monkeys the leader must constantly show that he is still the leader. So we tend to regard conflict as a way of establishing supremacy. This blanket supremacy will then enable our will to be done or will at any rate cow the opponent and make him more pliable. Instead of having to argue each case on its merits you establish that you are 'top dog' and thereafter your case is permanently endowed with rightness and good reason. There is a lot to be said for the practicality of this approach and there was a time (in the imperial days of Rome or Britain) when it worked marvelously well. Let us not knock it as an idiom but merely point out that it is no longer appropriate with today's weapons.

A union picks a fight with the management to show whose will is going to prevail. A government arranges a showdown with the miners' union in order to keep all other unions in order.

This is, of course, the macho view of a conflict. The substance does not matter, the dominance of winner over loser does.

ENJOYING THE CONFLICT

I have mentioned elsewhere in this book that the prolongation of a conflict may be in the interests of one (or even both) parties. It may be a matter of distracting attention from other matters. It may be a matter of creating an external enemy in order to create internal unity. It may be a matter of enjoying the importance a conflict confers. It may be that the reactive thinking of a conflict is more attractive to politicians because it is less risky than the initiative thinking required in peace. It may be that the press has so fired everyone up for the conflict that it has become a sort of sports fixture with a running score. We need to look closely at the perceived values of continuing the conflict.

CONFLICT POINT

There is an effort on both sides to crystallize disagreement on some basic point. Just as a successful advertising campaign must have a slogan, so a successful conflict must have a simple central theme. If the actual issue is complex then a simpler theme will be derived from it. Such slogans as the 'freedom of the individual' can usually be attached to any conflict. The other side, by virtue of what it is proposing, is threatening the freedom of the individual. This follows logically because if your side wants something and the other side has contrary wishes then they are seeking to inhibit your wants: your freedom of choice.

The important point is that in trying to solve conflicts we often go directly to the heart of the conflict which we assume to be this central point. This is a mistake. The central point is usually not the real reason at all but a communicable slogan.

If matters were not brought to this central conflict point then the conflict would probably not have arisen in the first place, since each separate point of disagreement would probably have been settled by discussion.

There is the notion — derived from the pre-antibiotic days of treating a boil — of bringing matters to a head. Once matters had been brought to a head then they could be dealt with. A conflict clears the air and sorts things out.

As mentioned earlier, the design approach to conflict resolution avoids this conflict point at first and only comes to it at the end.

WE CAN GET WHAT WE WANT

These are the initial days and the days of confidence. It seems likely that the outcome is going to go your way. Everyone in a race who has a chance naturally feels at the start of the race that the potential of victory is there. If we had a better way of assessing likely outcomes than the current one of the blank check of hope and wishful thinking, then fewer conflicts would be started. Perhaps there should be a skilled group of people whose job it is to assess likely outcomes (and costs, as I mentioned earlier).

False confidence and the euphoria of righteousness are always difficult to cope with. Timidity and caution are but weak words. We need a much stronger image to bring to mind the comparison between sensible behavior and the childishness of most conflicts. Perhaps we should practice going to the brink of conflicts we know we will never have in order to establish the value of conflict avoidance.

BACK OUT WITH SOMETHING

There comes a point, perhaps because of cost, when a party knows that victory in the original sense is no longer possible. At this point the party would like to back out with honor and with something to show for the cost and effort. It is at this point that the design effort is crucial. We just have to design both cosmetic and real benefits. Moving out of the conflict must now be a real opportunity, not a mere escape from disaster.

FORCED TO GO ON

We can be forced to go on: because our usual concept idiom is of victory and defeat; because we feel that the other party is in the wrong and must be punished; because the dialectic mode means that you can only be right if the other side is wrong. So we are reluctant to let the other party off the hook. He is on his knees: let us finish him off. The colossal reparations demanded of Germany after the First World War were unpayable, created horrendous inflation in Germany and were directly responsible for Hitler and the Second World War. The much more enlightened approach to Germany and Japan after the Second World War converted these two enemies into staunch allies.

The religious concepts of guilt and sin and punishment are out of place in conflict resolution. We need to show that a conflict is simply not a practical or effective way of getting something done. Unfortunately in many cases it is the only way because we have not designed better ways. So we need to do some design thinking about this.

Complete victory only makes logical sense because victory is assumed to be the end state of 'conflict'. There is no other reason why complete victory is important. Humiliation does nothing to improve the relations between the two sides and adds little of practical value.

NON-VICTORY OUTCOMES

It is perfectly possible for a party to go into a conflict with no intention of forcing a victory. There may be a range of other objectives. What may be desired is a compromise or even a permanent stand-off. It may be that the matter needs sorting out with some design.

The conflict may be the only practical means of energizing the system and getting something done. What is required is action, not victory. It is a pity the Argentinians did not signal this as their intention when they invaded the Falkland Islands.

There can also be a deliberate creep strategy. Here the purpose of the conflict is not to achieve final victory but to inch things forward. Campaigns for black rights and women's rights are of this type.

HANGING ON

The key question is whether a party is in control of the situation or just hanging on from moment to moment. The momentum of events may carry things along to such a stage where one party (and even both) are so locked into the situation that they can do no more than survive. They take whatever actions are necessary for the moment and hope that eventually things will sort themselves out.

This is a totally absurd situation where the conflict has become a sort of Frankenstein monster with all parties just serving its appetite.

It is very easy for an interactive situation to acquire its own life. This is because an interactive situation is not under the control of one party. The reactions of the other party are outside the control of the first party.

All the more reason for the parties to get together through an organization such as S.I.T.O. to take joint control of the situation again. No matter how valid the 'antagonistic' idiom might have been at the start of the conflict, once it has gotten out of control then a co-operative design mode is essential. If the boxing ring catches fire then both boxers co-operate to extinguish the flames.

PART V
STRUCTURES FOR CONFLICT RESOLUTION

CHAPTER 22

WHY EXISTING STRUCTURES ARE INADEQUATE FOR CONFLICT RESOLUTION

'I want you to design me the best possible racing car, according to the latest knowledge and research — ground effect and the lot. But it has also got to be suitable for my wife to go shopping in. You know, easy to park, good in traffic, easy to get in and out of, automatic transmission.'

'You want a sort of general-purpose machine that will do for Grand Prix racing or Saturday morning shopping?'

'No. I do not want a general-purpose machine. Such a machine would be quite good at each task and therefore quite inadequate at each task.'

'I'll design it for racing and then your wife will have to get used to using it for shopping — she won't like it.'

'You're fired. It must be possible to do it if I can sit here and specify what I want. I'll get another designer.'

The principle is obvious. If something is designed for one purpose it may simply not be much good for a different purpose. That is no fault of the structure or the designer.

There is a second principle. Saying that something is 'multi-purpose' does not *make it* multi-purpose. It may not be possible to have a multi-purpose structure even though one can specify it.

In this section I want to look at the existing structures for conflict resolution. At best they are inadequate, at worst they are positively dangerous and may actually exacerbate conflicts. In structure and in idiom they are part of our crude, primitive and antiquated approach to conflicts. I do not believe there is any hope of these structures changing their function or performance. They are locked in by the logic of their structures, the logic of their history and the logic of the people running them. They are also locked in by the logic of expectation: the need to continue functioning as people expect them to. In the next section I shall propose a new structure: S.I.T.O.

INADEQUACY

We can look at structures and find them inadequate for a particular task. It may be that they were never designed for this task. It may be that they are called upon to perform this task because there is simply no other way of doing it. I once had to iron a dress shirt with a frying pan wrapped in aluminium cooking foil — because there was no iron. It may be that the structure was adequate at one time but that the design of the structure inevitably led to a change in its nature, thus making it inadequate (as has happened with the United Nations). It may be that the nature of the task itself has changed. It may be that conflict resolution today is very different from what it was thirty years ago.

We often erroneously believe in 'general-purpose intelligence'. This means that an intelligent person can do anything. It also means that a group of intelligent people organized into a structure can direct its activities in any direction. This is a bad mistake. There is local logic and there are logic bubbles. The way an organization is designed will severely limit its general-purpose application. The structure of an organization is as real as the structure of a car.

If the only structures we have are inadequate then this means that conflict resolution will not be done very well. In such a vital area we do not have to tolerate inadequacy, nor should we put up with it. Conflict resolution is probably the most important area for the future of mankind and the continued existence of the world. Is it good enough to have it served in an inadequate manner?

COMPLACENCY

The big danger of inadequacy is complacency. If we have a structure that does a job rather poorly we may be happy with this because we *cannot imagine how the job could be done better*. This lack of vision and lack of understanding of human thinking is a severe handicap. The man who has no ambition and no vision of himself in a better job has to be complacent about his current work. There is nothing so blind as lack of vision. If we are really complacent about our existing structures it must be because we believe them to be wonderful — or we simply cannot envisage anything better. The whole purpose of this book is to suggest that there can be something better: both in the idiom of conflict resolution and also in a structure specifically designed for that purpose.

With complacency I am not just talking about the natural tendency of an organization to defend itself against charges of inadequacy. I would expect members of the organizations I shall mention here to protest that they are fully capable of carrying out the functions described in this book. That is to be expected. What is more dangerous is the belief on the part of others that an inadequate structure is adequate. This completely blocks the search for a better design. Motor car design has lagged far behind what is possible (in terms of materials, economy, safety, control, etc.) because everyone was complacent about the adequacy of existing designs.

DANGER

Here I am not referring to dangers of omission. The sheer inadequacy of a structure can lead to dangers of omission: things are not done simply because the structure cannot do them. I am looking at dangers of commission. The racing car used for shopping may not be good for parking: that is a danger of omission. But the fierce acceleration of the car may cause serious accidents: that is a danger of commission. Many of the structures we have that are concerned with conflict resolution not only fail to do the job but actually exacerbate matters and make them far worse. For example, the dialectic of democracy cannot help but be carried over into conflict thinking. We may not be too worried if our designed racing car does not win every race. But we should be worried if the shopping wife is slaughtering her fellow citizens in the high street.

STRUCTURAL LOGIC

I want to make it absolutely clear that my criticism of existing structures is not on the basis that they are run by incompetent people and that a change in morale and performance would solve the problem. Nor am I complaining that the thinking idiom employed is based on the inappropriate and incompetent argument mode. If that was all then some rigorous training might put things right. The complaint is much more fundamental. Just as a person has his or her own logic bubble, so a structure has its own logic. This arises from the purpose, structure and function of that organization. There is a logic of a racing car and a logic of a shopping runabout — quite apart from the skill of the driver.

If the U.S. Government runs a budget deficit (because of defense spending and because most government spending is locked in by legislation) then it may be the logic of the Federal Reserve to raise interest rates. This has a doubly harmful effect on Third World debtor countries. The deflationary effects of a high interest rate slow down economic recovery and the chance for Third World countries to earn money through exports and rising commodity prices. The higher interest rates the debtor countries have to pay to service their debts slow down their own productive investment. Yet the Federal Reserve and the U.S. government have a local logic that is primarily concerned with the U.S. economy and U.S. democratic elections. Indeed, the rest of the world is also directly concerned here because only a healthy U.S. economy can bring about recovery worldwide. So the structure of the situation creates its own logic. Again and again it needs emphasizing that part of the troubles of the world arise from man's inadequate thinking skills (and obsession with outmoded idioms), and part arise from his being caught up in structures which he himself has designed and is now slave to. There is only a guilt of innocence and a guilt of complacency.

THE UNITED NATIONS ORGANIZATION

I shall consider this first because this must seem to be the organization that was set up to carry out the functions for which S.I.T.O. is being proposed.

The idea of a forum of nations is a natural one and an excellent one. When we consider the failures and defects of the U.N. we should not overlook its very considerable successes and the fact that things might be very much worse if it did not exist. I am conscious of its excellences and it is against this background that I make my comments.

Since there is no conceivable single world authority it follows that any organization must derive its authority from a collection of member nations. If this includes all the nations in the world then the derived authority is complete. This is the traditional authority of the town hall or any democratic structure. It is the members that endow the organization with its authority.

In terms of conflict resolution there is a talking place where member nations can debate conflicts and potential conflicts. There are organizational channels for meetings and communication. Matters can be argued in private or in a public forum.

Should there be a need to condemn some wrongdoing on the part of a particular nation, then the U.N. passes a Resolution recommending that a certain action ceases (or takes place). This is the normal jury system of judgment. The force of this judgment derives from peer pressure and occasionally economic sanctions (with some policing role for U.N. troops). Largely it is peer pressure condemnation.

The jury system is the basis of the legal system in many countries. A group of people, with no direct interest in the case before the court, listen to the presentation of the case and then offer an opinion as to whether or not things happened in a certain way. The judge then administers the law.

The jury system can only work if the 'peers' are uninvolved in the case. In certain trials the selection of the jury takes a long time because jurors not only have to be uninvolved but also must not have any preconceived ideas or prejudices in the matter (derived from newspaper reading, ethnic background, etc.). Juror after juror may be rejected (in the U.S.A.) because a defense lawyer claims that the juror is not sufficiently detached.

Now in the early days of the United Nations this notion of a detached group of peer nations might have been valid. But as soon as nations form into real and de-facto alliances then the 'jury' concept is simply unworkable — it no longer exists. In the United Nations there are East/West power blocs reflecting the ideological conflict between the two superpowers. There are North/South alliance divisions along which Third World and developing nations vote against what they regard as the self-interest of the developed nations. There are specific alliances like N.A.T.O. The Falklands conflict was a classic situation in which two countries were caught in cross alliances.

As a N.A.T.O. ally of Great Britain and a co-believer in the need to prevent naked aggression, the U.S. had to support her ally. Because Argentina is in the U.S. hemisphere, because the U.S. is extremely sensitive about its image in Latin America and because some people in the U.S. administration believed in the merits of the Argentinian case (if not in the methods), the U.S. felt some obligation to side with Argentina. For Italy the conflict was between a European ally and fellow member of N.A.T.O. and a sympathy with the Argentinians since some 35% of that population is originally of Italian origin.

The very difficulty of these divisions indicates the existence of powerful voting alliances. On matters affecting Israel it is certain that the Islamic world will vote against Israel and that the U.S. (because of the powerful Jewish lobby and the U.S. commitments to Israel) will vote for Israel. All these are more or less permanent voting lines and are not issue-dependent as they might be with non-aligned nations. Indeed, non-alignment itself becomes a voting group where such nations will vote as a bloc against major power interests. It has all become some great quadrille in which groups form and reform according to the play of the music.

In short, the U.N. has become a sort of parliament or house of representatives. This has its own merits but it is quite emphatically no longer a jury system for the resolution of conflicts.

As I shall discuss elsewhere in this section, a parliament has grave disadvantages when it comes to conflict resolution. The parliamentary idiom is very simple. What our party advocates is automatically right. What the other party advocates is automatically wrong (and nonsense too). Matters can no longer be decided on their merits because party loyalty must come first. Whoever does not contribute to party loyalty on an issue (even against personal judgment) cannot then call on party loyalty in the future.

It hardly needs saying that once the idiom has switched to being that of a parliament the prevailing thinking idiom must be the inadequate and dangerous argument mode that I condemned earlier in this book. There is no other way to operate a parliament. Instead of constructive design there is attack and defense and the parading of righteousness. It also follows that much of the performance is not directed to resolving the conflict at all but to making an impression on other nations in the Assembly or in the outer world. It becomes a conflict *performance arena*. There are no elements at all of the needed design approach to conflict resolution that I am advocating in this book.

We could say that once the U.N. stopped being an independent jury system and became a parliament then it switched from having a conflict resolution role to becoming a sort of conflict *nursery*, in which conflicts could be seeded and nurtured as a way of extending and cementing alliances in the external world.

There can, of course, be no going back.

There is another aspect which I shall briefly mention here. Once the United Nations has passed a 'resolution' then it has taken a judgment stand in the matter. When the U.N. passed its resolution on the Falklands matter there was in effect a condemnation of Argentine action. Once a resolution has been passed then the U.N. can never be independent of its own resolution. It cannot be judge one moment and jury the next. Any neutral 'design' role of the U.N. is immediately ruled out by a resolution. The design aspects which I shall assign to S.I.T.O. (Supranational Independent Thinking Organization) in the next section could never be carried out by the U.N. after any sort of vote had been taken.

So we have to conclude that the U.N. is permanently structurally incapable of carrying out the design approach to conflict resolution. In a way this arises inevitably from its constitution as a representative body. Representatives have to represent their country otherwise they should be replaced by someone who will do the job properly. A representative cannot be independent of the interests of his or her country. Occasionally — as in the case of Jeane Kirkpatrick in the Falkland crisis — a representative is encouraged to put forward a different line as a way of permitting a country to be on two sides of the fence at once.

THE SECRETARY GENERAL OF THE UNITED NATIONS

To some extent the function of the Secretary General of the United Nations can be separated from the organization itself. The Secretary General is not directly representative, though the periodic election to that post does imply some dependence on those selecting the next person to fill the post. Even if the person is independent after election the election itself may reflect certain power bloc interests.

The Secretary General does have a certain mediation function simply because he is visible and is in a recognized authority role. He can act as a communication channel and can take initiatives in calling for meetings. The role is rather a low-key mediating role rather than the direct 'designing' role that I shall be advocating. The very fact that the Secretary General is called upon to do it strongly suggests the vacuum that exists — and the need for S.I.T.O.

It should be noted that the Secretary General has to act in a very personal capacity because he is only treated as a communication node. He cannot call on any official U.N. resources because this would immediately — and inevitably — be back with representative bodies. This would not be the case with S.I.T.O.

In effect, the role of the Secretary General of the United Nations is useful up to a point but very weak and derives not from any functional utility but simply from the existence of a communication channel where none otherwise exists. It highlights the need for something much more effective than the good will of an individual.

THE RED CROSS

As a neutral, independent and much respected organization, the Red Cross is in a very good position to play an important part in conflict resolution.

From time to time the Red Cross gets involved in such matters as the exchange of Israeli and P.L.O. prisoners. The Red Cross oversees adherence to the Geneva Convention. The Red Cross is prominent in relief work and humanitarian work of every sort. It is a remarkable organization and very effective.

The Red Cross consists of two parts. There are the individual Red Cross organizations in different countries. These are organized together as the Red Cross League which serves to co-ordinate the activities of the different independent Red Cross organizations. The other part is the International Committee of the Red Cross (I.C.R.C.) which is entirely Swiss and is based in Geneva. In times of war or conflict it is the I.C.R.C. which can act across national boundaries.

The I.C.R.C. is a non-representational body and therefore does not suffer all the disadvantages of a representative body which I mentioned earlier in this section when considering the U.N. The Swiss base is also an advantage inasmuch as Switzerland has a long reputation of neutrality and serves as home for many international organizations (in economic matters Switzerland is not neutral but firmly in the camp of the developed nations and also the capitalist economies — as contrasted with Third World countries).

It would be natural to assume that the Red Cross might enlarge its area of concern to broaden directly into 'intellectual humanitarianism' — in other words the resolution of conflicts through the application of human thinking. The Red Cross has no particular expertise in the area of thinking but it is well placed as a neutral independent organization.

It was this sort of consideration that led a Russian participant at the I.C.R.C. meeting held in Moscow in 1984 to suggest that the Red Cross should set up a small group to have a look at my work and at the S.I.T.O. concept. Such a meeting was set up in Oslo in July 1984 on the initiative of the Norwegian Red Cross. At that meeting it was made quite clear by Jacques Moreillon, of the I.C.R.C., that the Red Cross was extremely concerned about the reputation that it had built up over 120 years for humanitarian work. It was felt that any move into the 'intellectual' arena of conflict resolution could risk that reputation inasmuch as a party to a conflict might feel that the Red Cross had taken a position that favored the other side.

I respect this concern and I consider it very reasonable. There would always be such a risk if the organization was to work effectively in the conflict resolution area. This concern does, however, make it very clear that the Red Cross is not able to undertake the design approach to conflict resolution. That is all the more reason why there is a need for a new and specific organization like S.I.T.O.

The Red Cross will no doubt continue to act as a servicing organization to service those requests brought to it by nations for the carrying out of such tasks as the exchange of prisoners and other matters which are very closely related to its prime humanitarian task.

In a sense S.I.T.O. will have to function as an 'intellectual' Red Cross.

PRIVATE MEDIATION

On a quiet and very low-key level the Quaker group has for some time been involved in private mediation initiatives in such matters as the Biafra war.

This low-key mediation is very much in the nature of a 'lubricant' to oil the machinery of negotiation. For example, if the parties in conflict are not talking to each other then the Quaker representative would carry messages from one to the other as a go-between. He would seek to gain the confidence of both sides. He would seek to correct misperceptions and would try to explain the motives and position of one side to the other, on a personal and informal basis.

I have no doubt that this is a valuable function even though it does seem to be carried out on a rather *ad hoc* basis. Once again this type of activity does underline the need for a formal organization like S.I.T.O. which would exist in a permanently neutral and independent manner to provide a third party role in conflict resolution. It is possible that S.I.T.O. could support and co-ordinate the excellent efforts of those who are currently carrying out private mediation initiatives of this sort. There is certainly a need for more rigorous support of these matters (without losing the personal touch).

I should point out, however, that although S.I.T.O. may carry out go-between and 'lubrication' functions from time to time, this will not be the sole function of that organization. S.I.T.O. will not be concerned just to mediate in a conflict. In accordance with the concept of 'triangular thinking' which I have advocated in this book, S.I.T.O. will take part directly in the design of an outcome to the conflict. For this S.I.T.O. will be operating not as an errand boy between the disputants but as the organizer of the three-part team that is to set out to design the conflict outcome. This is an important point that needs making. Simply to provide a lubricating mediation service is *not enough*. That does indeed have a value but it is too weak. It leaves the combatants still locked into the combat mode. There has to be a much more active role in conflict resolution.

I have mentioned private Quaker initiatives here as an example of the private diplomacy that goes on. There are, of course, many individuals who for some years have been carrying out private diplomacy. They have built up contacts and credibility. Where it was to the advantage of their mission I would see such individuals working with S.I.T.O. which could act as a co-ordinating organization. In fact S.I.T.O. would want to call on the skills of such individuals for the carrying out of its task. One of the prime methods of operating of S.I.T.O. will be to call on resources of conflict-resolving skills wherever they may be found.

Let me repeat again that mediation is not the same as the third party role in the design of conflict outcomes. That is why it is useful to coin the term 'triangular thinking', since it implies a three-part design team, not just someone who holds the ring for the combatants.

GOVERNMENTS

Governments are simply not designed for solving international conflicts. Governments are designed for ruling a particular country. There is no reason to suppose that the requirements of this task are similar to the requirements of international conflict resolution.

For example, the extraordinary lack of continuity in the American diplomatic service reflects the government idiom of that country where a change in president (possibly every four years) leads to a total change in the administration. This system has many advantages because it gives change and hope and the possibility of bringing in talent from outside (in the British or Canadian system the country may be stuck for a long time with a group of wearying politicians with no hope of a quick change). From an international point of view this lack of continuity has destabilizing effects. Even in terms of personal relationships, on which trust is based, there must be problems with such lack of continuity. As I mentioned elsewhere, this must be contrasted with the extremes of continuity in the Russian foreign affairs departments.

President Nixon was perceived by the rest of the world as something of a hero in foreign affairs. He brought the Vietnam War to an end and opened up relations with China. Yet, within his own country, he was seen as something of a disaster.

Quite clearly the needs of internal government need not be compatible with the needs of international conflict resolution. For internal reasons and because of the way the media has to simplify matters for the public, governments seem to operate at international level a set of emotions that would not be out of place in a nursery. There is talk of 'friends' and 'enemies', of 'bullies' and 'evil monsters'. This would be utterly absurd were it not for the needs of the press and public. It should also be said (and I shall say it in more detail later) that this sort of language is the normal habit of democratic interchange. It is harmless enough when used within the family but gross when used outside the family.

I have mentioned at several places in this book that we should not always assume that both parties want to solve a conflict; a particular government may enjoy benefit from continuation of the conflict. Conflicts may serve as a way of distracting people from other matters; a way of creating an external enemy to blame for most things; a way of raising morale; etc. It is obvious that governments are not always interested in resolving conflicts even when they have not actually caused the conflict.

Any individual government that assumes a public conflict-resolving role is doomed to failure. There can be no real credibility. A major power will be seen as pursuing its own interests or those of its protégés. A minor country will be seen as presumptuous and pursuing the interests of minor countries. All countries are automatically seen as belonging to some power bloc or interest group: ideologically, economically, geographically or militarily. Even Switzerland, which is taken as such an exemplar of neutrality, obviously belongs very firmly in a particular economic camp and would never be seen by Third World countries as neutral in economic affairs. Indeed, the considerable fuss over the use of secret Swiss bank accounts to hide the funds of criminals or dictators is a good example of a clash between national interests and world morality.

Just as no individual government could have any credibility in a conflict-resolving role, so no group of governments could take up such a role. The reasons behind the grouping would always be suspect. It is quite obvious that any government is in place to serve the needs of its country. The best any government can do as its contribution to conflict resolution is to admit the inadequacy of existing structures and to give solid and visible support to an organization like S.I.T.O. which, by definition, can do things which no government can do (but every government benefits if these things are somehow done).

I want to come now to the effect of the type of government on conflict resolution.

DEMOCRACY AND CONFLICT RESOLUTION

Democratic governments have to get elected. Politicians and parties can take up certain attitudes if they feel that such attitudes will win votes. There is local logic in this. There is also the bubble logic of individual politicians fighting for election or for prominence within a party. Tough positions are more visible electorally than compromise, negotiation or conflict resolution. The idea of walking tall and carrying a big stick is part of our emotional culture. To be strong and not to use that strength is a universal ideal. That way you cannot be pushed around. That way you can defend yourself. There is nothing wrong with this gentle giant idiom. But it has to be carried through. That means a spending on defense. It means talking tough all the time and acting tough from time to time. The threat of toughness is much more practical than its exercise. It is expensive to have to prove, in combat, that you are tough. So it is much better if everyone knows it because of your stance and gestures. The animal kingdom knows this well. Dominant animals will threaten and gesture to indicate that actual combat is not worth the effort since defeat is likely.

All this makes a lot of logical sense both in itself and also in terms of winning votes. If one side restrains itself from these advantageous noises then the other side will take advantage of the unused idiom.

Every democracy would like the dual-level communication that I have mentioned at various places in this book. One level of communication for home consumption and one level for international affairs. The concept is intuitively grasped by most leaders but proves extremely difficult to operate in practice, since any seeming lack of sincerity is quickly apparent (especially on television). You cannot call someone a bastard unless you really seem to mean it.

When we come to actions rather than talk then the luxury of two levels is not possible. If you send troops to Grenada you send troops to Grenada. You cannot ask someone to believe that you have not sent troops to Grenada.

It is perfectly true that democracy can act as a control on aggressive tendencies. The U.S. withdrawal from Vietnam was a democratically mediated groundswell of opinion. The opinion was probably not against being in Vietnam (although it would be positioned this way) but of being involved in a war which could not easily be won — therefore making the sacrifice of life pointless.

In general, however, once a conflict has been declared there is a tendency for democracies to close ranks in a bipartisan approach. Anything else seems very close to treason. To sabotage the war effort of your country is sabotage. Not to support the troops who are risking their lives for your country is shameful.

A country may need the firm leadership and determination of a Reagan or Thatcher. The decisions of such leaders arise more from a sense of style consistency than from consideration of each situation, as I described in an earlier section, and this can be dangerous from an international point of view. What would Mrs Thatcher do if a slightly different Falkland Islands problem arose with a larger country — perhaps Spain and Gibraltar?

There is no reason at all to believe that any democratic leadership represents the wisest or cleverest brains in a country. It may represent the best politicians, but that is a different matter. Many intelligent people have neither the skill, the stomach nor the need for power that is required of a politician (we can also add idealism in some cases). Even amongst politicians the skills of getting elected are not at all the same as the skills of government. So we have a situation where the best brains are not brought to bear on those major conflicts which demand the very best brains available. An organization such as S.I.T.O. would be able to tap such resources wherever they arise, independent of party coloring.

It might also be said that because of the self-organizing nature of perception (as I described in an early section), no convinced party follower could really make the best use of his or her own brain power because the world has to be viewed though the party line — and a good brain will be able to make a good rationalizing job of it.

I have mentioned many limitations of democracy with regard to international conflict resolution. We come now to the most basic limitation. The thinking mode of democracy is — and for the foreseeable future will be —the classic argument mode. You are right and the other side is completely wrong. The style of thinking and appropriate noises accompany the performance of party conflict. It is quite unrealistic and absurd to assume that people immersed in the practice, and adoration, of this idiom will suddenly be able to cast it aside in order to adopt the 'design' approach to conflict resolution. At very best they will be able to achieve the lawyer style of negotiation and mediation. This is a sort of compromise and value trading. It lacks the creative and constructive effort that is the basis of design. With design you may move outside the given frameworks, instead of analyzing and arguing within them.

BUREAUCRATS

Every bureaucrat has a very clearly defined logic bubble. He or she is selected because of a match with the existing culture of the organization. Bureaucrats want to operate the system according to the rules and procedures because this is the universe of action — and in time they may move from being the guardians of the rules to the designers of new rules. There is an unwillingness to be visible. At all costs visible mistakes are to be avoided. The simplest way to do this is to stick to the rules and, where possible, to pass the buck to someone else. Many problems will go away or lose their intensity if time is used as a positive weapon.

The rewards for initiative and enterprise are so vastly outbalanced by the penalties of failure and mistake that no intelligent bureaucrat will so contradict his or her logic bubble as to be entrepreneurial. Even a successful enterprise creates enemies and risks promotion on the basis that promotion comes to 'sound people' who do not take risks with innovations.

None of this — in any way — is a fault or deficiency on the part of bureaucrats. In my experience they are highly talented people. They are intelligent enough to play the rules of the game as they are written by the nature of bureaucracies. Survival is what it is all about — as it is in politics.

So when we look at institutions or organizations that might play a role in the resolution of conflicts, we have to consider to what extent such

179

organizations are energized by bureaucrats. If this is the case there will almost certainly be a lack of that design enterprise that is required for conflict resolution. In setting up any new organization, such as S.I.T.O., this is a danger that will have to be avoided.

The thinking style required for *administration* is quite simply not the thinking style required for *enterprise and design*. This is seen very typically in the administration of large philanthropic foundations, where the necessary bias towards administration can completely kill the social enterprise role which must be the sole justification for such foundations: to pioneer things that would otherwise never be pioneered.

CENTRALIZED GOVERNMENTS

I include here all those types of government where decisions are taken centrally. There may be democratic election processes but these are not open to the general public but confined to party members. The spectrum may span from socially responsible administrations trying to do their best for the population to classic dictatorships. The only reason these diverse forms are considered together here is that politicians do not have to make electoral promises to get elected and that there is a certain security and continuity of power.

Obviously such systems do not suffer from the many disadvantages that I listed when considering democracies. There is more continuity. More able people may be in power. There is less dependence on the argument mode. There is no need to curry favor with an electorate which might be less than sophisticated in certain matters. It could be said that such governments are actually in a better position to resolve international conflicts than democracies. There are, however, some defects.

With centralized governments, internal power plays become very important. Within the party structure there may be jockeying for position. For example, a military faction may take control or may offer its support to one or other group. Any power group in command has its own priorities, its own perspective and its own way of doing things. It had to be a military government to take the Falkland step. Lack of dissent may mean that it is difficult to get a broader view or alternative views of a situation. There is usually a firm hierarchy of values and therefore less interplay of values in different situations.

With a democracy, mistakes are usually fatal to a government or an individual. Mistakes are therefore avoided. The downing of the Korean airliner would have had colossal repercussions if it had happened in the

U.S.A. In a democracy politicians have always to be looking over their shoulders at how the public will react. In general this can be a sobering influence to restrict any wild adventures. In some cases it can encourage belligerent attitudes. But belligerent attitudes are even more easily encouraged in a charismatic dictatorship.

To be fair, it should be said that if a centralized government sincerely put its mind to conflict resolution it could probably be more effective at it than a democracy. This follows because any centralized government has more power for good and more power for evil. It was the purpose of democracy to strike an average: foregoing some of the good in order to avoid much of the evil.

THE VATICAN

There was a time when the Vatican could play a third party role in conflict resolution. This was when most of the squabbling nations (in Europe) were Catholic and therefore accepted the authority of the Vatican. The Vatican was perceived to be neutral and to be superior to local national interests — at other times it was a very direct player in temporal power plays. The Vatican drew the line that stopped Spanish and Portugese fights over new territories. This is why the Brazilians are alone in South America in speaking Portuguese for they fell one side of the line. Even today the Vatican is trying to settle the dispute between Argentina and Chile over the Beagle Channel.

Today, the Vatican still commands a sort of supranational respect but the ideological divide puts it firmly in the Western camp. In addition, the enlargement of the 'known' world now includes such significant players as China, with a quarter of the world's population. The natural authority of the Vatican does not automatically extend that far.

It is, however, worth noting two points about the historic Vatican involvement. The first is that the Vatican acted at a senior level — as a partner in conflict resolution, not as a low-level errand boy. This is the type of third party role that I have been advocating in the book under the term 'triangular thinking'.

The second point is that the Vatican existed as a *special state* in its own right. It owed allegiance to no one. Sometime in the future we may actually create a mini-state as a sort of focused intellectual haven whose citizens were not subject to patrial pressures. That would be an ideal setting for the S.I.T.O. concept.

Such a concept is not impossible once we realize the immense importance of human thinking and the contribution it is going to have to make to the future of the world. It was probably a fatal mistake to site the United Nations in New York.

SUMMARY

There is a vacuum. There is a gap. There is a need. In this section I have tried to show that we simply do not have the structures necessary for the resolution of conflicts. This is not through any ill will or incompetence. It is simply that structures designed for a specific purpose may be inadequate for other purposes.

I have explained why the United Nations organization cannot perform the third party role in the design of conflict outcomes. Its representative nature rules this out because of different allegiance groupings. The Red Cross is too virginal about its reputation and a tightly perceived sphere of operations. Individual governments cannot carry out the role because of lack of independence and because any government has a first duty towards its people. The International Court at The Hague can only deal with strictly defined legal matters. Private diplomacy will always have a role to play but it is too weak and too 'errand boy' in nature to play a positive design role. The Vatican can no longer perform this function.

So we need a new structure to carry out in a practical way the design approach to conflict resolution. This is to be contrasted with the argument approach to conflict resolution.

If we do not perceive this need and if we are too complacent with regard to existing structures then we show a remarkable lack of vision.

In the next section I shall lay out the S.I.T.O. proposal.

The whole of the book is really a leading up to this concrete proposal. Criticism of an existing state of affairs with a concrete alternative is misplaced confidence in the ability of a system to improve itself.

CHAPTER 23

S.I.T.O.

We come finally to the most important part of the book: the practical method for putting into operation the concepts expressed in this book. If our traditional argument idiom is inadequate for conflict resolution and if our existing structures are ineffective for this purpose, then we need something new.

The new thinking idiom is the designed outcome idiom. The new structure for applying this idiom is S.I.T.O. The emphasis will be on creative design, not on dialectic clash.

In this section I shall outline the nature and function of S.I.T.O. It is not important that I go into great detail. The value of the S.I.T.O. concept arises from the *direction* it indicates. Something like S.I.T.O. is absolutely essential. What I shall put forward here are proposals as to structure and function. But the value of S.I.T.O. does not depend on these particular proposals. It may be that the final form will be very different. Matters are still at the shaping stage. At this stage there is a need for input from those parties who would eventually be making use of S.I.T.O. for conflict resolution. How would S.I.T.O. be of most value to them? How could S.I.T.O. avoid those pitfalls which experience has shown to weaken conflict resolution initiatives?

A beginning has been made. S.I.T.O. has been established as a foundation in The Hague with an initial operating base at Palazzo Marnisi in Malta (a small, neutral and non-aligned country).

The S.I.T.O. initials stand for Supranational Independent Thinking Organisation.

SUPRANATIONAL

S.I.T.O. needs to exist and to function outside politics, ideologies and nations — as a sort of intellectual Red Cross organization. It is not an international organization but a supranational one. It will not be a representative body like the U.N. and there will be no member nations either in the governing body or as voting delegates. I have explained the reasons for this fully in an earlier section. Any representative body can never act independently of the wishes of the representatives, who in turn cannot be independent of the interests of their own countries. This would completely destroy the purpose of S.I.T.O. which is set up specifically to get away from this limitation. S.I.T.O. is positioned as a supranational body and will act as one.

INDEPENDENT

S.I.T.O. must be free of any allegiances or dependencies. In particular it cannot have any continuing paymaster. If S.I.T.O. is dependent on a particular paymaster then its actions will always be interpreted as being influenced by that dependence. The United States has withdrawn from U.N.E.S.C.O., which indicates that that body is expected to satisfy its member states, and if it does not do so any member can withdraw its financial support. S.I.T.O. must be free to work on conflict resolution without any suggestion that certain parties must be pleased. Unless the thinking of S.I.T.O. is seen to be independent then it is worth no more than the partisan thinking of which there is already so much at the moment. S.I.T.O. must be independent of votes and of continuing financial support. Individuals who contribute their thinking to S.I.T.O. will do so as individuals. Though S.I.T.O. will happily co-operate with existing bodies like the U.N. and the Red Cross, it will at all times maintain its independence of thought.

THINKING

The main purpose of S.I.T.O. is to provide a body which will focus *directly on thinking*. This is what is special and unique about S.I.T.O. There are bodies which focus on national interests. There are bodies which focus on special areas such as agriculture or health. The purpose of S.I.T.O. is to focus directly on thinking. It is true that the thinking of S.I.T.O. will be directed to conflict resolution (amongst other things), but it will always be the contribution of thinking to conflict resolution. For this reason S.I.T.O. cannot simply be a grey administrative organization staffed by bureaucrats. The emphasis on 'thinking' means that such a body can only be set up by people who have special experience in this field.

ORGANIZATION

An organization is more than an individual. It is more powerful and more effective. It has continuity and it has amplifying possibilities. I do not think that the conflict resolution concepts put forward in this book can be effectively applied unless there is an organizations structure to apply them. S.I.T.O. must exist in its own right. It cannot be a matter of just calling in a consultant no matter how talented. A consultant is always a sort of servant. S.I.T.O. has to have its own authority and to come in as a partner in the triangular thinking concept. S.I.T.O. must be able to take initiatives, set up task forces and organize conferences. S.I.T.O. must be able to prepare and publish reports. It will also be a value of S.I.T.O. that it can act as an umbrella organization to co-ordinate individual diplomatic efforts. The organization must be slim and effective rather than bureaucratic and empire building.

NAME AND LOGO

The name S.I.T.O. is designed to be pronounceable in most languages (English, Spanish, Japanese, etc.). The sounds used show the least variation in different tongues.

EXISTENCE VALUE

The first value of S.I.T.O. is that it should exist. In an earlier section I indicated that a concept had to come into existence as a 'concept'. A general descriptive phrase or exhortation was perfectly usable for communication purposes but could not function as a concept. Consider the following description:

> 'We have not developed very effective ways of resolving conflict. We tend to rely on the argument mode which is a continuation of the conflict. We need to move towards a 'designed outcome' mode which consists of exploratory mapping followed by creative design. Our present bodies for conflict resolution are structurally inadequate and we need some new body to put into effect this different approach.'

That is a lot to think of each time and even more to say. The whole paragraph can, however, be encapsulated as the S.I.T.O. concept.

Thereafter it can be referred to as such. It becomes possible to talk about the S.I.T.O. approach to conflict resolution. It becomes possible to contrast the argument mode with the S.I.T.O. approach (designed outcome, triangular thinking).

Once a concept has come into being as a 'node' in perception then experience can start to organize itself around that concept. It is like the first houses that spring up at an important road junction. Once they are there then a small village develops and eventually a town. Finally it is a significant town with suburbs and a network for communication to other towns.

So the very existence of the S.I.T.O. concept provides a focus point and a starting point. It becomes possible to think in this direction. It becomes possible to think in terms of an alternative to argument. It becomes possible to think of third party roles, triangular thinking and designed outcomes. A new road direction shows that the old road is *not the only one*.

LEVEL OF OPERATION

I have made clear throughout this book that the designed outcome approach to conflict resolution requires a three-part design team. That is the notion of triangular thinking. S.I.T.O. acts as the third party and as an overseer of the thinking involved (as in the normal drawing of a triangle). I have made clear that the thinking element in conflict resolution is the key element.

I have made clear that I do not have in mind low-level mediation, messenger or errand-boy functions (valuable those these may be). Nor do I have in mind the normal concept of negotiation as a bargaining procedure. I have tried to make it quite clear that the design mode is different. As with any design process the clients have the right to reject the final design, but during the design process the designer is not the servant of the client.

This point is very important because it affects the whole success of a design approach. If a mediator is regarded purely as someone who can help out the combatants then there will be no real attempt to design an outcome. The combatants and their thinking remain in control. For the design idiom to work the design idiom has to take control — for the moment. A home owner who calls in an interior designer and then proceeds to tell the designer what to do will get no true value from the designer and a resulting mess. Any worthwhile designer would simply walk out because no design is possible under such conditions. It is the role of the client to provide the brief and the input as required. Finally the client can approve the ultimate design.

In the case of S.I.T.O. the clients will be part of the triangular design team but all three parties will be working together.

STRUCTURE OF S.I.T.O.

There will be a small central secretariat that will deal with administration, organization, communication and the preparation for meetings. The role of this secretariat will be one of support to enable the whole organization to operate.

A central council will provide a core team of thinkers who believe in the S.I.T.O. concept, are skilled at the design approach and have experience in the field of conflict resolution. Some members of this team will be more actively involved than others.

Within each country there will eventually be a National Committee which will organize and carry out S.I.T.O. functions in that country. It will also be the function of that National Committee to identify and communicate with thinking resources in that country.

S.I.T.O. will build up a *resource field* of thinkers who will always operate as individuals and who have shown a skill in the design approach to conflict resolution. On any occasion such individuals may be tapped as a 'thinking resource'. This can be done by involving them directly in a design team or by seeking their contribution on defined thinking tasks. There is no limit on the size of this resource field.

NATION INVOLVEMENT

The support and involvement of nations is of great importance to the S.I.T.O. concept. Nations have to see S.I.T.O. as being of value to them in their conflict needs. I have already had indications from several nations that they see a great value in the S.I.T.O. concept. As I mentioned earlier, it will be important to work with different nations to shape the eventual form of S.I.T.O. I also hope that smaller nations and Third World countries will see that S.I.T.O. offers a unique opportunity for input that does not depend on military or economic power.

S.I.T.O. will not be a representative assembly. Nevertheless each nation will be asked to assign a specific S.I.T.O. delegate who will act as the liaison and communication point for S.I.T.O. matters. In addition a nation would specify a thinker who could be called upon to represent the views of that nation.

It is expected that national governments will see the value of having S.I.T.O. as an independent body and yet co-operating closely with it — as now happens with the Red Cross.

OUTSIDE VIEW VALUE

The parties involved in a conflict simply cannot look at that conflict from an outside view. No matter how intelligent they are or how objective they try to be, it is simply not possible to be both inside a conflict and also outside at the same time.

S.I.T.O. will be ideally placed to provide such an outside view. This is a value that arises directly from the existence of S.I.T.O. as an independent body. In practice it is not always easy to obtain an outside view because friends are not really outside the situation and journalists have a particular angle to cover. Who do you ask for an outside view? There is as yet no formal structure for this. S.I.T.O. will provide such a formal structure.

CONVENIENCE VALUE

I want to deal first of all with the value of S.I.T.O. simply as a *convenience* to parties involved in a dispute. This convenience value arises because the mere existence of S.I.T.O. allows the parties to do things which could not otherwise be done. I want to emphasize that this function is quite separate from the main *design* function of S.I.T.O. This convenience function does not in any way depend on the exercise of useful thinking skill by S.I.T.O. The mere existence of S.I.T.O. suffices for the convenience purposes.

S.I.T.O. can provide a channel for communication where none otherwise exists. For example, the British could have been talking to the Argentinians through S.I.T.O. This function is similar to a normal mediation function.

S.I.T.O. can offer an *oblique* way of putting forward probes, proposals and suggestions (as I have mentioned earlier). A party to a conflict may not wish a suggestion to come directly from its own mouth. The suggestion can be fed to S.I.T.O. who will put it forward as a S.I.T.O. probe.

S.I.T.O. can provide the auspices for a conference or meeting when neither side will accept the other side as the host. S.I.T.O. can be used for pre-preliminary meetings, such as summit meetings, when neither side is willing to issue a direct invitation for fear of rejection.

A party to a conflict may realize that it is in a losing position. Instead of losing to the other party, it may be preferable (from a face-saving point of view) to accept a S.I.T.O. recommendation.

Initiatives in general can be channeled through S.I.T.O. rather than put forward by either side in a dispute.

In order to defuse a situation that has escalated to a crisis point, the matter could be referred to S.I.T.O. as a 'cooling-off' measure.

S.I.T.O. could be asked to prepare a 'conflict report' as a basis for negotiations.

S.I.T.O. could be asked to organize a third party view on a set of proposals.

These and other similar functions can be seen as having a convenience value to the parties involved in a dispute. None of these situations depend on any special thinking talent on the part of S.I.T.O. In none of them does S.I.T.O. get involved in its true role as outcome designer. Nevertheless they offer a real value for S.I.T.O: a value which must be apparent even to those who doubt whether the design approach can offer any benefits over the traditional argument approach. The convenience value alone could justify S.I.T.O. And once in existence S.I.T.O. could demonstrate the other — more important — values.

EXPLORATION AND MAPPING

We come now to the real purpose of S.I.T.O.: the provision of a type of thinking that might not otherwise take place in conflict situations. In an earlier section I described the exploration or mapping type of thinking. This makes use of deliberate attention-directing tools. They serve to 'unbundle' thinking so that instead of the need to maintain the argument position there can be a mapping of the whole situation. It would be the role of S.I.T.O. to supervise and carry out this mapping exercise, working with the conflicting parties separately and also together.

It would be normal for a mapping exercise to proceed to a full-scale design effort. The mapping exercise does, however, have a value in its own right and it is possible to stop at this stage. The conflicting parties would now have a clearer view of the situation, of their own position and of the position of the other side.

This mapping exercise has to be supervised by a third party even though the actual thinking will be done by the conflict parties. It is possible to make a mapping effort from within a particular conflict position but it is much less efficient than one supervised by a third party.

CREATIVE DESIGN

This is the main S.I.T.O. role and the one that has provided the theme for the book. Instead of the argument mode there is to be a designed outcome mode. Any conflict is to be regarded as a design opportunity. In the full exercise of

189

'triangular thinking', S.I.T.O. will work with both parties as a three-part design team to create a designed outcome. As I have mentioned several times, S.I.T.O. will work as an equal member of the design team but will also orchestrate the thinking: defining creative tasks and setting the agenda.

It should be noted that the purpose of the design effort is to come up with an acceptable designed outcome that makes sense to both parties.

It is also part of the design effort to produce a range of alternatives at any point. There is no limit to the creative alternatives that can be produced and it is absurd to suppose that the parties in a conflict can generate all the possible alternatives. The value of an alternative is that it enriches the perceptual map. Even though it may not be used it can have an influence on how things are considered. Once thought, an additional option can never be *unthought*. It remains permanently available as part of the map.

Even less defined than alternatives are what I have called 'suggested directions for solution'. These are no more than directions which thought could take. They are by no means complete ideas. But once a direction has been set then thinking can move in that direction (like the Wright brothers setting the direction of 'unstable planes').

The harvesting of the creative effort is also an important S.I.T.O. role. Every creative effort has a useful outcome — if only we are trained to harvest that outcome. It is quite wrong to suppose that a creative effort has been a waste of time if it has not produced the ultimate designed outcome.

Even when there is a designed outcome this can usually be improved upon or indeed exchanged for a better one. Design is a continuous process. Nevertheless it is not possible to sit around and work towards the ultimate idea. Action may have to be taken. As in manufacturing, the design may have to be 'frozen' so that it can be used.

It goes without saying that a design is not just an abstract utopia. The conditions for acceptance of the design; the transition steps; the edge effect; the implementation procedure are *all parts of the design*. These are not things which are just added on afterwards. Indeed the design of a transitional step may be the most important part of the design.

In this creative design aspect S.I.T.O. could work in one of two ways. The main way would be for S.I.T.O. to work directly with the parties involved in the conflict in the operation of triangular thinking. S.I.T.O. could also tap its thinking resource field and also set up a separate thinking task force to design alternative approaches to the conflict. There could be occasions when S.I.T.O. would take this route even when it was not directly involved in a conflict.

PROBLEM SOLVING

Although this book has been focused on the creative design approach to conflict resolution, there are other areas that also require creative thinking and the new concepts and perceptions it brings with it. These might be specific problems or just concern areas. They could include unemployment or Third World debt. These are areas where S.I.T.O., with its independent thinking role, could provide an input, for example by organizing concept review conferences (as I shall explain later).

A conflict is a particular type of unsatisfactory situation. It happens to have a crisis quality and can also be both damaging and wasteful. That is why we need a better approach to conflict resolution. It also happens that the argument approach is inadequate. So this book is about the design approach and about S.I.T.O. as a means for providing this approach. The application of thinking is, however, broader than this.

CONCEPT REVIEWS

There is information and there is detail and there are concepts. Concepts are ways of organizing other concepts in order to provide convenience of description or in order to make things happen. We can have the risk-spreading concept of insurance. We can have the concept of value added tax. There is the concept of 'tax' itself. Some countries, like Singapore, have a concept of forced saving which is part tax and part saving.

A concept review takes place at concept level. What are the available concepts in this situation? What concepts are weakening? What are the dominant concepts? What are the changing concepts? What new concepts are beginning to emerge? What concepts are blocking progress? What are the concept needs (areas where we need a concept but do not yet have one)? A concept review presents the present situation in such terms.

A concept review may be presented as a report. There could also be a Concept Review Conference where people met precisely to examine the concepts in a particular field. S.I.T.O. could be involved in setting up such conferences. It would do so in partnership with an organization that was expert in the field. S.I.T.O. would provide the thinking framework and concept emphasis. The expert organization would provide the area expertise.

AUSPICES

S.I.T.O. can take the initiative in setting up meetings which can then take place under the auspices of S.I.T.O. There may also be other bodies that are established under the general umbrella of S.I.T.O. For example, the permanent U.S.A./U.S.S.R. Council mentioned earlier might be such a body. Once S.I.T.O. has established full credibility in its focus on thinking then this credibility can be put to work in a number of ways.

CONVENTION

S.I.T.O. may get involved in putting together a sort of Geneva Convention of conflict discussions. This could be a charter which would be signed by various nations. The putting together of such a charter would itself be the subject of a conference. The contents of such a charter might include the following:

1. That early in a potential conflict a signatory country would send a delegation to meet with an opposing delegation under the auspices of S.I.T.O.
2. That both parties would continue in permanent discussion even at the height of conflict or war.
3. That no 'walk-outs' or abstentions would be permitted.
4. That S.I.T.O. would be called in to help design a conflict outcome even if only one party desired this.
5. That there would be a periodic publication of positions and changes in position as seen by S.I.T.O.
6. That each party should make a statement of values, principles and fears.
7. That there should be a definite statement of offers that were still on the table.
8. That an updated compilation of alternatives should be permanently available.
9. That abusive language and terminology be excluded from S.I.T.O. discussions.
10. That objections must be spelled out in detail and not applied on a blanket basis.

There could be many more. The purpose of a convention is that it converts unproductive behavior into an obvious 'sin' instead of having to condemn it from moment to moment. People know what they should be doing and what they should not be doing. A convention also stabilizes a framework.

METHOD OF OPERATION

There are four basic ways in which S.I.T.O. will operate.

1. The 'full operation'. S.I.T.O. will work with the parties involved in the conflict as a three-part design team to design an outcome to the conflict. There would be the classical triangular thinking. The parties involved would come to S.I.T.O. and the design exercise would take place on S.I.T.O. territory. This is important because the whole tone and idiom of the discussions might have to be different from the argument mode that was present before. Such a change of mood and context would not occur if the disputants stayed in the same setting. It is preferable that the disputants come to S.I.T.O. rather than that S.I.T.O. goes to the disputants. In the latter case S.I.T.O. would be operating as a mere consultant. In the former case S.I.T.O. has the role of prime designer.

2. The 'parallel operation'. Here the S.I.T.O. involvement is set up in parallel to whatever other means are being undertaken to resolve the conflict. The S.I.T.O. operation parallels these other efforts. In this case the S.I.T.O. effort does not take over completely. Both parties will have to put together delegations that would then meet with S.I.T.O. It could even be that the involved delegation pauses in its other activities to take part in a S.I.T.O. session and then returns to direct negotiation.

3. The 'review operation'. Here S.I.T.O. attends conflict discussions as an observer. The observer reviews what has been happening and from time to time provides an input that may consist of this review together with such other things as alternatives and suggested solution directions. The S.I.T.O. role becomes one of additional input.

4. The 'direct operation'. S.I.T.O. can act on its own account. It can call conferences, publish reports and set up task forces to consider issues and conflicts. S.I.T.O. does not have to wait to be asked. S.I.T.O. can use its thinking resource field to design conflict outcomes. The outcomes will be published and will provide visible options that become available to those taking part in the conflict. These parties can take note of the outcomes and the public can also take note.

There are times when S.I.T.O. will act in a highly confidential manner. At other times S.I.T.O. may act in a highly visible manner. This all depends on the needs of the situation and the involvement of the conflicting parties. The decision as to the choice of high or low profile would, of course, be made at the beginning. It goes without saying that confidential information would never be disclosed. There are times when disclosures are to the benefit of the parties involved. For example, there can be 'kite flying' or a 'leak' of a possible outcome in order to prepare the ground. Secrecy has its value and so does visibility.

TRAINING

One of the roles of S.I.T.O. might be to establish training systems for the training of negotiators in the thinking methods advocated in this book. This will always be worth doing in its own right. Nevertheless such internal training will never be able to supplant the value of an independent third party role — as provided by S.I.T.O.

It would be immensely useful for all those involved in conflict thinking to have some understanding of the designed outcome approach.

FUNDING

This is a difficult point because any continuing S.I.T.O. paymaster would destroy the concept of independence. Ideally the funding should be of an endowment type.

The colossal cost of conflicts should serve to put into perspective the modest funding required for the S.I.T.O. operation. The needs would be for people costs and support costs. As I mentioned earlier, the U.K. miners' strike is estimated to have cost about £10 million a day or £3.5 billion in all. The Falklands War probably cost about £2 billion (possibly a great deal more) with residual costs for Britain of £600 million a year. A single F-18 warplane costs about $22 million. A single day of serious combat would cost a minimum of $50 million. It is against this background that we must consider how much we want to spend on conflict avoidance. If every nation were to allocate just 0.01% of its defense budget to conflict avoidance this could result in a huge saving of money.

S.I.T.O. STYLE

It is very important that S.I.T.O. is seen to have a clearly defined style. Such a style would include the following elements.

There would need to be ruthless intellectual honesty. This would have to lead to detachment and objectivity. Things would have to be seen in relation to widely differing value systems.

There would be an abstinence of judgment as regards value judgment. As regards prediction (will it work) and fit (does it serve its purpose) there would be the normal judgment of the design process.

There should be a richness of alternatives. Even when some of the alternatives are less attractive than others, they should still be visible as part of the concept repertoire.

There should be the provocation of new ideas, new perspectives and new solution directions.

There should be close attention to benefit, value and opportunity.

There should be close attention to edge effects, transition steps and the practical implementation of ideas.

There should be an emphasis on the acceptance of the designed outcome.

There must be clear and comprehensive mapping of the situation.

In general S.I.T.O. should operate in a style of clarity and definition. There should not be waffle and tentativeness. S.I.T.O. must orchestrate and lead the thinking rather than just drift along with it. S.I.T.O. must develop its design authority.

CREDIBILITY

It has to be a chicken and egg situation. S.I.T.O. has to start functioning in order to show its value. But until it shows its value it is difficult to start functioning. As a concept, S.I.T.O. arises from the inadequacy of our current conflict resolution systems. We have to be very complacent indeed about these in order to deny the need for something like S.I.T.O. We can take the defeatist attitude that our conflict-resolving methods are as excellent as they can ever be but that conflicts are simply insoluble because of human nature. This ignores the fact that our existing conflict-resolving structures (never mind the thinking) are not adequately designed for conflict resolution.

If we are happy with our conflict-solving methods then we are in for a very bad future.

It may take time for S.I.T.O. to build up its credibility, value and design skills. I am, however, convinced that this direction needs to be taken. And if not now, then when?

The important point is that what comes out of S.I.T.O. depends entirely on the investment which we are willing to make in S.I.T.O. If we believe that it can help then it will help. It is a direction we dare not ignore.

In the end the dilemma is a simple one: if the parties involved in a conflict are not in the best position to design a way out, then how should this be done? S.I.T.O. is an answer.

The costs of conflicts can be so enormous that even some improvement must be worth having. We can expect considerable improvement once we realize the inadequacy of our usual conflict thinking.

There can be no more important matter for the future of the world than conflict resolution.

EPILOGUE

There are those who will say that the aggressiveness of human nature, the arrogance of faith and the urges of power will always lead to conflicts on the what-you-can-get-away-with basis. There are those who will say that the only real security is a defense tough enough to deter an aggressor. Nothing I have written in this book disagrees with those views. That has not been my purpose.

I have claimed that our conflict thinking is a limited form of thinking that exacerbates conflicts and makes them difficult to solve even when both sides are really interested in a resolution of the conflict. I have suggested that we need to shift from the argument/clash mode to the design mode. When you set out to design an airliner you have to take into account different values (range, load, fuel consumption, safety, noise, seating, comfort), different principles (aeronautic and economic), and different interests (operators, passengers, producers and environmentalists). Yet in the end the plane must *fly*. The design approach to conflict resolution is similar. There are different values, different principles and different interests, but the outcome must *fly*.

Once we have set our minds to designing an outcome for a conflict then we have to use the appropriate thinking. The argument/clash mode is simply not a design mode. That must be very clear. We use the argument/clash mode for lack of anything else and because the parties involved find it impossible to switch from the conflict idiom to the design idiom (they are locked in by their positions).

The design mode *demands* a heavy creative input. It is not just a matter of dealing with the available concepts and perceptions but of creating new ones. There is a need to create new options. Argument can do this only to a very limited extent.

The purpose of S.I.T.O. is not to provide instant solutions but to provide a *focus* for precisely this design type of thinking with its creative needs. In practice S.I.T.O. could be used in one of three ways. S.I.T.O. could be used as an 'ingredient' in any conflict resolution process that is already underway.

197

S.I.T.O. would seek to provide new options and new possibilities. Once a thought has been put on the table it can never be unthought. The second way is when a conflict might be referred to S.I.T.O. for a designed outcome. Both conflicting parties would then appraise this outcome. The third way is for S.I.T.O. to act independently to set up 'concept review' conferences and reports.

There are two points which I must keep emphasizing in order to prevent a misunderstanding of the role of S.I.T.O. The first point is that negotiation is *not* the same as design. Negotiation is a give-and-take bargaining between the conflicting parties. Design starts from a basis of the whole field — in which the two parties are factors along with many other factors. The second point is that S.I.T.O. is not there to function as mediator, negotiator or judge. The specific role of S.I.T.O. is that of creative design with the emphasis on 'creative'.

It will be said that the conflicting parties would never listen to S.I.T.O. because S.I.T.O. has no power base. There are two answers to this reasonable objection. The first is that S.I.T.O. is there to provide *value* not power. A vitamin pill has no power. S.I.T.O. is intended as a help and as a resource — to be used as needed. The second answer is that S.I.T.O. would always have the 'power of ideas'. Once a perception is seen to have value then power flows from that value (as in the case of Christianity and Marxism). Finally there is the power of referral: if a conflict is referred to S.I.T.O. then S.I.T.O. can provide a design opinion.

It is not the purpose of S.I.T.O. to provide instant solutions to all the world's problems. The value of S.I.T.O. is to provide a way of focusing creative and design thinking on these problems. The ultimate value of S.I.T.O. will arise both from its own work and also from the way others perceive the value of such a resource.

I do have to say that none of the objections that I have ever heard amount to a sufficient reason for not proceeding with the project. The potential benefit (upside) is immense and the dangers (downside) are nil. What is needed is vision, courage and implementation.

Although this book leads up to the concept of S.I.T.O., the bulk of the book exists in its own right. I have set out to show that we need to shift from the argument/clash approach to conflicts to the design approach. For that we need some new thinking.

INDEX

and Korean airliner 181
politics of 60
problem-solving in 39
road deaths in 64
and teaching thinking 29
Texas 154
and U.N.E.S.C.O. 150

Values 58, 63–65, 110
  direction in 64
  taboo 63
Vatican 181, 182
Venezuela 13, 29
Victim 110
Victory 161/2
Vietnam 77, 158, 176, 178
Voting 104, 171

War
  in Biafra 174

in Falklands (see Falklands)
economics of 157/8
historical scale 1
nuclear 2
surrogate 149
in Vietnam (see Vietnam)
World War I 159
World War II 49, 94
Water shortages 26, 88
Watergate 78
Wedge, thin end of 145
Whittle, Frank 21
Wisdom 56
Workers 118
Working backwards 88
Wright Brothers 115

Zero base budgeting 105